THE DAYS OF JAMES IV OF
SCOTLAND

THEN AND THERE SERIES
GENERAL EDITOR
MARJORIE REEVES, M.A., PH.D.

The Days of
James IV of Scotland

WILLIAM STEVENSON, M.A.

Illustrated from contemporary sources by

H. C. McBEATH

LONGMAN

LONGMAN GROUP LTD
London
*Associated companies, branches and representatives
throughout the world*

*First published 1964
Second impression 1965
Third impression 1970
SBN 582 20400 3*

FOR HELEN

ACKNOWLEDGEMENTS

For permission to include drawings based on copyright sources
we are indebted to the following: the University of Glasgow –
page 1; the Duke of Norfolk – page 85. In addition we wish to
express grateful thanks to Mr. E. F. D. Roberts of the National
Library of Scotland, Miss Patricia M. Ford of the Royal Scottish
Museum, Edinburgh; Mr. J. G. Scott, Curator, Department of
Archaeology and History, Kelvingrove Art Gallery and Museum,
Glasgow; and Mr. A. Fenton and Mr. S. Maxwell, both of the
National Museum of Antiquities, Edinburgh, who have rendered
valuable assistance in the preparation of much of the material.

PRINTED IN MALTA BY
ST PAUL'S PRESS LTD

CONTENTS

LIST OF PLATES

On Monday, 11 June 1488, near the town of Stirling, and beside a little stream called the Sauchie Burn, two armies formed up to face each other before joining battle. Even at a distance, it would have been possible to tell the names of the nobles who commanded in each army from the standards which added splashes of colour to the flash and glitter of the arms and armour on each side; but, conspicuous among them all, was the red and gold banner of Scotland, and, strangely enough, it was being carried by both armies! It floated over King James III of Scotland, where he sat on a great grey horse and looked doubtfully at the army of the rebel nobles which faced him, and exactly the same standard waved above Prince James of Scotland in the centre of a bodyguard of these same rebels, where they took their position behind the *vanguard*[1] of their army.

Soon the trumpets sounded and the rebel army advanced: the hum of arrows filled the air and the Borderers shouted loud and fiercely as they clashed with the King's vanguard. But King James made no attempt to lead his own army forward and, when the loyal nobles suggested that he should leave the field and find a place of safety, he quickly wheeled his horse out of the press of men and galloped away towards the east, hoping to take refuge on Sir Andrew Wood's ships, which lay in the Firth of Forth.

No doubt Prince James was glad to see his father leave

[1] You will find words printed like *this* explained in the Glossary on page 100.

King James III

the dangers of the battlefield, for he had given strict orders
that no one in the rebel army was to harm him, but he
could not have known that that was to be the last time
that he saw his father alive. As the King galloped at
flight speed through the village of Bannockburn he was
thrown from his horse and carried, semi-conscious, into
the mill, where, a short time later, one of his enemies – no
one knows who – *masquerading* as a priest, was brought to
him, whom the King asked to give him the *sacrament*.
'That shall I do hastily,' said the man, and stabbed
James to the heart.

So, at the age of fifteen, Prince James became King of Scotland, and we are told that, ever afterwards, he wore an iron belt or chain to which he added a few links each year in *penance* for the part that he had played in his father's death. But, in spite of this poor beginning, James was destined to rule over Scotland for the next quarter-century, into which are crammed many most interesting and important events, and to die at the head of a Scottish army in that country's most famous defeat.

The Royal Crown of Scotland

Life and Work in Those Days

What was Scotland like in those days long ago when James was her king?

Would we have enjoyed living in his reign?

We shall have to leave the answer to the second question until we know the answer to the first; so let us try to find this, first of all by looking at the descriptions of the country written by two people who were alive in James's reign.

The first of the two was a clever Scotsman called John Major, who, after studying at Cambridge and Paris, became principal *regent* at the College of Glasgow, and, later, the *provost* of St Salvator's College at St Andrews. He was also the author of a book called A HISTORY OF GREATER BRITAIN, and it is from this book that we get some of our information.

John Major lecturing

I

The second was Don Pedro de Ayala, the Spanish Ambassador in Scotland, who, on 25 July 1498, wrote a long letter to King Ferdinand and Queen Isabella of Spain, telling them about the country, about the King, and about the people themselves.

Unfortunately, we cannot accept all that these two writers say as being absolutely true, because John Major was out of the kingdom for a large part of James's reign, while Don Pedro painted a glowing picture in order to try to get the King and Queen of Spain to agree to a marriage between James and a Spanish princess. But, if we are careful, perhaps we can succeed in getting a picture of Scotland that is not too far from the truth.

First of all, there is no doubt that Scotland at the end of the fifteenth century was a poor country – even Don Pedro says so – though it had improved greatly from the time in 1435 when a traveller in the country spoke of '. . . the poor, who almost in a state of nakedness begged at the church doors . . .': and who said that bread was eaten '. . . only as a dainty'. Most Scots people lived by farming, but, though both our writers say that there were many cattle and sheep, their estimates of the actual numbers may not be accurate. Both Major and Don Pedro also agree that the country was famous for the quantity and variety of the fish and shell-fish that were caught in its streams and around its shores, and they mention salmon, trout, turbot, pike, herring, oysters, crabs and lobsters. Dried fish, called stock fish, were exported to European countries, along with skins and hides, wool, some cloth, and, strangely enough for such a poor country, large pearls! Do you know where these would be found? People still fish for them in the same place today.

The most important person in the country was, of course, James himself, for, though Parliament met eleven times during his reign, it was a very different body from the Parliament that we know today, and usually it was just asked to agree to decisions which had already been taken. Of course, the King had his Council to help him, but it was he who had the last word in everything and even had to see that the laws were carried out after they were made. He spent much time in riding round the country to make certain that justice was being done to everyone and that lawlessness was being put down, especially in the remote Highlands and in the unruly Border country. Perhaps Don Pedro was right when he said that it was because of his energy in this direction that James had much less trouble with the great nobles of the kingdom than his father had, for it seems to be true that the Scot at this time was a quarrelsome fellow and had to be kept in order pretty strictly. If two nobles of equal birth lived near each other, John Major said, arguments and bloodshed were common.

What was he like, this King on whom so much depended?[1] We know already that he was hard-working and active and could keep the nobles in their place – but let us listen to Don Pedro:

> 'He is of noble *stature*, neither tall nor short, and as handsome in complexion and shape as a man can be. His *address* is very agreeable. He speaks the following foreign languages: Latin, very well, French, German, Flemish, Italian and Spanish. . . . His own Scottish language is as different from English as *Aragonese* is from *Castilian*. The king speaks besides, the language of the savages who live in some parts of Scotland and of the islands. . . . He is well read in the Bible and in some other devout books. . . . He never cuts his hair or his beard. It *becomes* him very well.'

(But he did so after his marriage to Margaret Tudor: perhaps she did not like it as well as Don Pedro!)

[1] See plate facing page 24.

'He fears God and observes all the *precepts* of the Church. . . . Rarely, even in joking, a word escapes him that is not the truth. . . . He is neither *prodigal* nor *avaricious*, but *liberal* when occasion requires. I have never seen a man so *temperate* in eating and drinking out of Spain. Indeed, such a thing seems to be superhuman in these countries. . . . His deeds are as good as his words. For that reason, and because he is a very *humane* prince, he is much loved. . . . James possesses great virtues and few faults worth mentioning.'

That description makes the King sound like a very nice person, doesn't it? Even though we know that Don Pedro must have exaggerated a bit, James must still have been very attractive to both old and young, for we read how once a poor child came up to him and took his hand and was given a gift of 3*s*. and again of another time when he gave 14*s*. to a woman with five fatherless children. The account books of the Lord High Treasurer have many of these little acts of kindness written down in their pages, and they would certainly help to make James the popular King that he was – but we must let Don Pedro finish his description, for in the last part he is foretelling the future, without knowing it himself.

'He is courageous, even more than a king should be. . . . I have seen him often undertake most dangerous things . . . I sometimes clung to his skirts and succeeded in keeping him back. On such occasions he does not take the least care of himself. He is not a good captain, because he begins to fight before he has given his orders. . . . He said to me that his subjects serve him with their persons and their goods, in just and unjust quarrels, exactly as he likes, and that therefore he does not think it right to begin any warlike undertaking without himself being the first in danger.'

As we shall see at the end of the story, James told Don Pedro the exact truth: but neither could have guessed that James's eagerness to be the first into battle was going to cost him his life on a wet September day seventeen years after that conversation.

Lastly, let us have a look at the people of Scotland as they appeared to our writers. Just as they are today, they were then divided into Highlanders and Lowlanders, though John Major calls them the 'wild Scots' and the 'householding Scots'. The former, which included the inhabitants of the islands, spoke 'Irish' – that is, Gaelic – and they were very agile and warlike people. Don Pedro, who saw them fight, said that they did not know what fear was. Their dress was a *saffron*-dyed shirt and a loose plaid; they carried a bow and arrows, a broadsword and a small *halbert*, and they had a single-edged dagger in their belts. In war-time, the better-off Highlander fought in a leather coat sewed over with iron rings, but the common people trusted to a patchwork linen garment covered with *pitch* or wax, and a deerskin overgarment. One part of these wild Scots had large flocks of sheep and herds of cattle and horses, and kept the laws fairly well; the other part had bad leaders, and lived by hunting and by making war on their neighbours.

Armed Highland warrior

The lowland Scots spoke English and were also divided into two classes, country-dwellers and town-dwellers. The former rented their land from the nobles and it was cultivated by their servants: they were almost as warlike as the Highlanders, took their lords' quarrels as their own, followed them in battle and thought that work at a craft was beneath their dignity. For this reason, they looked

5

Scots hunting in the mountains

down on the town-dwellers, who were regarded as unfit for war because they lived quiet lives and ate and drank more than was necessary. Altogether, it would seem that Don Pedro had some excuse for saying that the Scots spent all their time in war, and, when there was no war, fought with one another!

But, before we begin to look at some of the interesting happenings in James's reign, let us examine a little more closely the life of these people in the country and the towns.

THE LIFE OF THE PEOPLE: THE COURT AND THE CASTLES

We will start with the King himself, and, in order to see Scotland at its most picturesque, we will visit James and his court at Linlithgow Palace[1] during the Christmas festivities. The accounts of the Lord High Treasurer of Scotland tell us a good deal about the way King James kept Christmas, for, of course, all the feasting and enter-

[1] See plate facing page 25.

6

tainment had to be paid for, and a record had to be kept of what money was spent, and in what ways. If we were really able to transport ourselves back in time, it would be quite easy for us to see all that was going on at the palace, for the doors were always open to all those who cared to come and join the Christmas celebrations, whether it was the great lords who got special invitations to come to the 'Kingis Yole' (*Yule*), or the strolling players, tale-tellers and *minstrels* who knew that they would be welcome at this time

A fifteenth-century jester

because they could amuse the King and the court.

The holiday period usually lasted from St Nicholas

A tapestry

7

Day (6 December) until Twelfth Day (6 January), and about a week before Christmas itself a line of laden carts would rumble out of Edinburgh and move westwards towards Linlithgow. They carried the *tapestries* and other hangings which were to cover the walls of the hall, the silver vessels for the table, the furniture for the chapel, the cupboard (on which the plates and *goblets* were displayed),

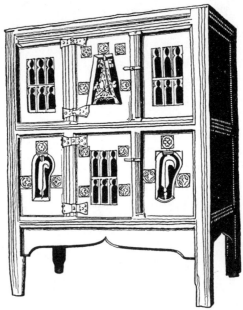

A cupboard made about 1500

and all the many other articles which were necessary for the comfort of the King and the court. The removal of so much furniture (and sometimes even windows were taken too!) from one dwelling to another for a short visit seems strange to us, but there were several reasons why it was done. First, the court never stayed long in one place, for the King had to travel round the country eating up the

8

food which formed part of the rents paid for the royal lands. Also, plumbing was poor in the fifteenth century, and, after the court had been in one place for a few weeks, the drains had to be cleaned out and new grass and rushes spread on the floors. Thus, it was not worth while having every royal palace fully furnished, and so most of the necessary furniture moved when the King did, either in carts or on pack horses. This shortage of furniture is one of the things that we would have found odd in James's reign, and it is quite startling to find that Darnaway Castle

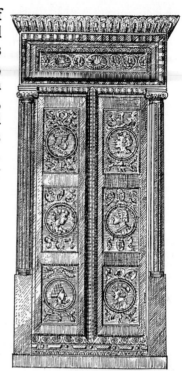

A carved oak cabinet

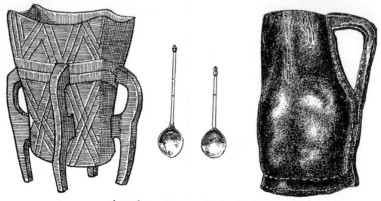

A mether, *spoons and a leather jug*

in 1505 contained little more than the following list:

One folding table with two leaves.
Two beds with red and green *canopies*.
Six feather mattresses and two bolsters.
Six pieces of tapestry.
One chair, three forms and five tapestry-covered cushions.
Forty-six plates and dishes and one *charger*.
Twelve *trenchers*; four pots; four pans; two iron *spits*; two *cauldrons*.
Six candlesticks; three leather jugs; and eight ale barrels in the cellar.

A sixteenth-century candlestick

I am sure that we would consider a modern house to be very poorly furnished if it did not contain a good deal more than that castle.

As soon as everything was prepared at Linlithgow, the King, accompanied by some of the courtiers, would leave Edinburgh and come riding through the winter darkness towards the welcoming lights of the Palace. In preparation for the arrival of the royal party, Thomas Shaw, the King's cook, and his assistants would be labouring mightily in front of the roaring fire in the kitchens, for, though James was not a big eater himself, his followers would be sure to be ready for a good meal after their seventeen-mile ride from the capital. The trumpeters would blow a welcome as the *cavalcade* clattered across the drawbridge and into the courtyard, and, a short time later, they would all be standing round a bright fire in the great hall.

Before the meal was served the guests washed their hands in the basin which was carried round by a servant,

Fireplace in Linlithgow Palace

whilst another followed the first with a *laver* or *ewer* of fresh water. Then the King and the principal guests would take their places at the 'high board', the table which stood on a *dais* at one end of the hall, while the less important sat down at side tables, all with their backs to

A laver and basin

the walls so that the opposite sides of the tables were left free for service from the centre of the hall. Heralded by savoury smells, the meat would arrive from the kitchens to be carved for James and his guests by the King's carver, ready for them to eat with the help of their fingers and their knives. The main course might be one of a number of different meats. *Venison* was served very frequently, but the *swan, heron, bittern* and *solan goose* also appeared, as well as *sturgeon* and *porpoise* and even seal meat – a whole seal was bought for 5s. at Linlithgow in 1491, and may have been eaten at the royal meal. For the second course there might be a large variety of dried fruits, and the food would be accompanied by wine from France or Germany sweetened with sugar, as it was then rather bitter.

Firelight and candle-light were the only means of illumination. The flames would flicker on the plates, goblets

and bowls brought from Edinburgh to grace the table and the cupboard, and glint redly on the eyes of James's favourite dogs where they waited hopefully for scraps among the rushes and the sweet herbs that covered the floor. The familiar tapestries would sway gently in the draughts from the ill-fitting windows, and the subdued hum of talk would blend with the music of a handful of musicians and singers who stood in the shadows at the end of the hall.

A sixteeth-century chair, made in France

Then, the meal being

over and hands again washed, the dining-tables would be removed from the *trestles* and leant against the walls, and James's guests would draw their benches nearer the fire, while the King sat in his own chair, covered with red velvet and fringed with silk. Everyone would relax in the warmth and in the knowledge that it was the start of the holiday, and, though the minstrels and pipers were ready to entertain James and his friends, the thought of rest and sleep would soon break up the company before the fire.

The bed on which the King slept must have been a rather splendid affair, for we know that no less than 32 *ells* of brown shot silk were used to make a covering and a roof for it, 12 ells of *buckram* went to line the roof, and 8 ounces of silk were used to sew all this cloth and to make fringes! The blankets in those days were made of *fustian*, a

A late sixteenth-century bed

coarse cotton fabric, or of broadcloth, and the sheets were of linen, while over the pillows was spread the 'head-sheet', made of linen, silk, fur, or even cloth-of-gold, with a similar 'foot-sheet' at the other end of the bed. There were curtains on the bed too, made of different coloured silks and decorated with cloth-of-gold and cloth-of-silver. (You can see a sixteenth-century bed-curtain[1] in the Royal Scottish Museum in Edinburgh.) We do not know if James's bed at Linlithgow had a 'futegang' – a long step or stool which was made like a box so that clothes could be kept inside it. If there was no futegang, then there would be a chest for clothes, but no other furniture.

As Christmas approached, the usual gifts of cloth for new *liveries* were given to the members of the court, and the palace must have been colourful indeed when everyone dressed up in their new clothes. There was David Cald-

[1] See plate facing page 25.

Fashions about 1450

14

well with a gown of brown English cloth, and Willie Crichton and Tom Pate dressed in red gowns and hose and blue doublets; James of Whitelaw and eight *yeomen* of the stable were all in green, while Downie the *falconer* and Long Tom, his man, were decked out in grey. As if by contrast, Andrew Wood and James Sinclair were all in black, both having received four ells of 'French black'; while James himself was as colourful as any of his subjects, with a crimson satin 'side gown' and a long gown of velvet lined with *damask*, and two black satin doublets and one of crimson, all specially made for Christmas, 1489.

While we are talking about clothes, it is interesting to know that laws had to be passed setting down what each class of person was to wear. For example, the common people, labourers and husbandmen, were to wear white or grey on week-days and light blue, green or red on holidays, and the cloth for their garments was not to cost more than forty pence per yard, which meant, of course, that silks and satins were forbidden. On the other hand, the Lords of the Parliament were to wear a *mantle* of red cloth, lined with silk or furred with grey, green or purple stuff, and furred hoods of the same cloth on their shoulders. Scotland seems to have been a much more colourful country in these days, at least as regards clothes!

Christmas Day itself began with a carol sung for the King by the Chapel clerks, and then, some time before midday, preceded by the heralds and *pursuivants* and attended by his court, James went to High Mass and made his Christmas offering, which might be anything from 14s. to 28s. On the way back to the palace or in the hall at noon, the heralds cried '*Largesse*' to the King, as was the custom, and received a gift which might be as much as £10, while the trumpeters got about half that amount. After the Christmas dinner, the rest of the day was spent

St. Michael's Church, Linlithgow

listening to the music of the harp or the fiddle, watching
the dancing of 'gysaris' (mummers), or seeing a play,
perhaps by Patrick Johnson and his Linlithgow players, or
a Nativity scene by the Chapel clerks. If these amusements
were not enough, there was card-playing or dice, or
Currie, the court fool, dressed in the red and yellow coat
given him by the King as part of his wages, would entertain the courtiers with song and dance. Then, as the
evening got late, Watschod, the tale-teller, might be called
for, to grip the attention of King and commoner alike
with some story of heroism or adventure in times long past,
while the Highland harpers who stood among the per-
formers plucked chords on their instruments to suit the
mood of the story.

The person in charge of all these amusements had a number of rather odd names. He was sometimes called the Abbot of Unreason – you can guess why – but in Aberdeen he was the Abbot of Bonaccord, so called because of the city's motto, and in Edinburgh he was sometimes known as the Abbot of Na Rent, perhaps as a sly dig at the real *clergy*, to whom the people had to make various payments, as we shall see. It was usually a young member of the household who was chosen to be the master of the revels, but sometimes a person of importance was chosen, and was glad to

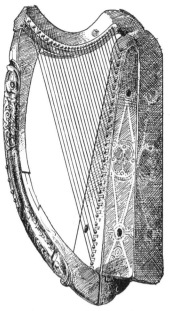

A clarshach or Highland harp

pay a fine to escape doing this duty, for it demanded hard work and must have needed a lot of energy and invention. We can tell that the revels were often boisterous, as in 1496 the sum of £10 was paid to Gilbert Brade of Stirling to repair the damage done to his house by the Abbot; and in 1503, even the King himself had to pay up to get back his *pitcher* which had been taken by the Abbot, who, on this occasion, was Alexander Kers, James's own cook.

The end of Christmas Day was certainly not the end of the Yule celebrations, and New Year's Day was often the time for giving presents rather than 25 December, especially the gifts called 'basin silver', which were presented by the King to some of his servants, such as Robert Douglas, the keeper of his wine cellar, who got £10 in 1507. Here is a little list of gifts, written just as it is in the Treasurer's Accounts – see if you can understand all that it says, and work out how much James gave altogether to these musicians.

	£	s.
Item, to the Italien schawmaris,[1] v Franch crounis,[2] summa[3]	III	x
Item, to the fiff[4] Franch menstrales,[5] v Franch crounis, summa...	III	x
Item, to the sex trumpettis, vi Franch crounis, summa ..	IIII	IIII
Item, to Guilliam, taubronar,[6] and his man and Adam Boyd, iiii Franch crounis, summa		lvi
Item, to Adam Dikeson, Thomas Jestour, tua[7] piparis[8] of Edinburgh		lvi
Item, to ane[9] menstrale of the Erle of Bothuiles		xiv
Item, to ane gret cumpany and divers[10] othir menstrales	xxv	xvi

1. *Players of instruments like an oboe.*
2. *crowns*
3. *total*
4. *five*
5. *minstrels*
6. *a drummer*
7. *two*
8. *pipers*
9. *one*
10. *various*

Can you work out how much a French crown was worth in these days?

At last, 6 January – 'Uphaliday', as it was called – came round. On the evening before, the King or Queen of the Bean was chosen by cutting the Twelfth Night cake and finding who had the slice with the bean in it. It was then his or her duty to preside over the festivities of the next day, the real King '*abdicating*' for a few hours in favour of this new ruler of the revels. With these celebrations the holiday period came to an end, and the King – the real one – and his court went back to the hard daily work of governing the kingdom.

18

THE COUNTRY

Now that we have seen a part – and the easiest part – of the life of the court, we will go almost to the opposite extreme and see how the ordinary *peasant* of sixteenth-century Scotland lived. One of the things that we noticed in the last section was the lack of furniture and the discomfort of the castles of the time, but if we think that the castles were bare and draughty, then to us the houses of the peasants would be rough and rude indeed. Andrew Simpson, one of the tenants of the royal lands in Stirlingshire in 1500, could have told us all about them!

In Scotland at this time it was common to find the *arable* land divided up into what were called 'plough-gates' of 104 Scots acres each. These, in turn, were divided into smaller pieces called 'oxgangs' or 'bovates' of about thirteen acres each; two of these bovates formed one 'husbandland'. In some places, therefore, each peasant (or 'husbandman') might have two of these oxgangs, and might contribute two oxen to the common plough. But we must not imagine that the whole country was divided up neatly into ploughgates and oxgangs, all exactly alike, and the farm on which Andrew was a tenant was one of the many exceptions to the rule.

It was called the Grange of Bothkennar and it contained $27\frac{1}{2}$ bovates (or $357\frac{1}{2}$ acres) which were divided between eleven people. Andrew had one of the largest shares, 4 bovates or 52 acres, and probably this farm was something of a family affair, as there were four other Simpsons working on it – Thomas, John, William and Alexander. But though Andrew's neighbours, David Kincaid and Alexander Muir, also had 4 bovates, William and Alexander Simpson had only 2, and Thomas and John had $2\frac{1}{4}$ each. Thus, we cannot say that there was any special way of dividing the land and nearly every farm was different. As we know, in those days rents were not paid entirely in money, and on Bothkennar each tenant paid 16s., about 5¼ bushels of grain, twice that amount of flour and 2 capons for each bovate of his holding. By using the little table on page 25, can you find out roughly how much the total rent was for the whole farm?

As well as paying this rather odd rent, tenants often had to do extra work on their lord's lands, especially at the busy times in the farming year, when they had to help with ploughing, sowing and harvesting. They also might have to give 'short carriages' and 'long carriages', which meant transporting various kinds of goods, such as cheese, salt, coals, slates and lime for short or long distances. They were also 'thirled to the mill', which meant that they had to have their corn ground at the mill owned by their lord, and they had to pay him for allowing it to be ground there, and they had to pay the miller for doing the actual work. Both the landowner and the miller were usually paid in grain, and this might amount to one-eleventh of the peasants' whole harvest. If they were forced to use another mill because 'their' mill was out of action, they still had to pay their own miller the usual charge, and they often had to help to keep the mill *lade* in repair and to bring millstones from the quarry, which might be a long distance from their homes. As if this was not enough, when the tenant of an oxgang or more of land died, his lord could claim his best animal from the tenant's heir. This was an old custom called '*heriot*': and as a '*corpse-present*' or '*mortuary due*' the parish priest could take his second-best animal or the tenant's best garment.

Andrew and his neighbours rented their land for three years at a time, and when they renewed their leases at the end of the three years they had to pay a '*grassum*' (a sum equal to the money part of the rent) to the King before they were allowed to do so. Because they held their land for such a short time, and because they were so poor, they did not think it worth their while to build big houses – in fact, we should probably have called them huts, not houses at all. They were built by erecting two beams, called '*cupples*' in the form of a capital V upside down at a certain distance from a similar pair: the two pairs were then joined along the top by a long beam called the 'roof-tree', and other beams were added for support. (You can draw a diagram of this for yourself.) Then low walls of turf or stones were built, and the roof was made of poles laid from the roof-tree to the top of the walls, and covered with heather or sods. Doors were made of wickerwork or an ox hide, and window openings were closed at night by wooden shutters or by the skin of an animal. In many of these poor buildings the fire was in the middle of the floor, and, of course, a hole in the roof would take the place of a chimney. As you can imagine, the house would be filled with a smoky haze all the time. The few cattle which the

A 'cuppled' house

tenants possessed occupied the same building as their human masters, perhaps separated from them by a small partition of wickerwork, and the hens roosted at night among the cupples above their heads. In such a house it would be impossible to keep oneself clean, but the people did not seem to mind. 'The *clartier* the cosier', they said!

We do not know what these smoky, evil-smelling dwellings contained in the way of furniture, but probably not more than a few stools or blocks of wood for seats round the fire, perhaps a bed of some sort, but more likely a pile of straw and skins in a corner, and a few rude wooden dishes for the daily meals. These consisted largely of milk, oaten bannocks cooked on a stone in front of the fire, and meat, venison and fish, the second and third of these only in those parts of the country where they were easy to get. As we know, fish were plentiful, and John Major says that 100 herrings could be bought for a *liard* – an old French coin worth 3*d*. – and a large fresh salmon for 2*s*. Of course, peasants such as Andrew Simpson could not afford to spend as much as 2*s*. on a salmon, for all their money had to be saved up for their rent, and few were as fortunate as those who lived near Major's home on the south side of the Firth of Forth, who were able to catch the solan geese on the Bass Rock. The young were eaten and their feathers were sold, while daring men could even climb to their nests and get the fish which the birds had caught in the sea for themselves. But we are probably quite safe to believe the writer who said that, though the Scots ate bread only as a dainty, they ate fish and flesh 'to *repletion*'.

Not only were the houses very different from present-day farmhouses, but the farms themselves were unlike anything we can see today. There were then no fields surrounded by hedges or stone walls, but only patches of arable land among the rougher ground; this arable land was divided into two parts, called *infield* and *outfield*. The infield was the better land and crops were grown on it all the time; the outfield was poor land, a part of which was cultivated for a few years until the soil was exhausted, when another part was ploughed up and planted. The tenants' holdings would be divided up among these patches of infield and outfield in the form of strips or *rigs*, each shaped like a long capital S, and separated from the one on either side by a *balk* of stones, grass and briars. This was known as the 'run-rig' system of farming, but not all the land was divided in this way; some tenants had their holding in one compact piece, while others rented not only the land but the cattle and the farm implements as well, and promised to give them all back again when they ceased to rent the land. This was called 'steelbow tenure'.

The farm work was often done by a team of neighbours working together, for the farm implements were usually owned by all. We have already seen that each person was expected to supply one or two animals to the common plough, which was so heavy that it required about eight animals to pull it and perhaps four men to help – one to drive the team, one to guide the plough, one to hold it steady in the furrow and one to ride on it to add extra weight, though heavy stones tied to the plough might be used instead.

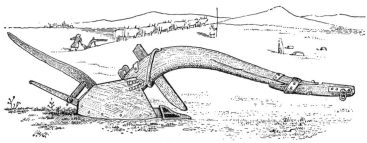

Old Scots plough

Cutting corn with a sickle (a later picture)

The corn was cut by *sickles* and the grain was beaten out of the husks by *flails*, after which it was *winnowed* to separate the corn from the loose husks. This was often done on the top of a hill on a windy day so that the husks would be carried off by the breeze when the mixed heap was tossed in the air. The grain was then ground in a water-mill, or by a *quern* or hand-mill if the water-mill was out of action.

The cattle were very small and thin, and many of them had to be slaughtered before the winter as there was so little food for them. (Parliament passed Acts ordering the people to plant broom, which was mashed up and fed to the cattle, as there was so little hay.) Both John Major and Don Pedro speak about the

A flail

A quern for grinding grain

24

King James IV of Scotland,
1488–1513

Queen Margaret, daughter
of King Henry VII of
England

The Watson Mazer, also made in the sixteenth century, now in the Royal Scottish Museum

A sixteenth-century bed curtain, like the one mentioned on page 14

The Palace of Linlithgow, one of James IV's favourite residences

big flocks and herds to be found in Scotland in James's reign, but, of course, you will understand that these animals were much smaller than those of the present day. Major explains that an ox could be bought for 2 francs (£2 Scots, or about 12*s*. in English money), and a ram for about 1*s*., and when he says that the price of a fat capon was half that amount, it gives us a good idea of the size of the ram.

Thus, we can see that life for Andrew Simpson and all other Scots peasants was a constant struggle to grow and gather in the crops on which they depended so heavily; and that a harvest failure could mean not just hunger, but absolute starvation for all.

OLD SCOTS GRAIN MEASUREMENTS
6 Firlots (bushels) = 1 Boll.
16 Bolls = 1 Chalder.

(But different counties had different sizes of measurement, and even the standard measures were badly made and not accurate.)

THE TOWNS

In such a poor country as Scotland in the sixteenth century, we should not expect to find any large towns or cities, but at this time it did contain thirty-nine royal *burghs*. These burghs were the most important places in the country, for they possessed certain rights and privileges which other places did not have, such as the right of choosing their own *magistrates*, punishing wrong-doers and settling disputes in the burgh courts, of holding weekly markets and annual fairs, and of charging *tolls* on goods brought into the burgh by outsiders. As you can guess from the name, these rights were granted to them by the King, and, though other towns might also get some of these rights, only royal burghs could engage in foreign trade (take part in a 'wild adventure', as it was called), or send representatives to Parliament. Of course, there were great differences in the size and importance of these burghs, for, though some of them had been founded in the reigns of David I, William the Lion or Alexander II or III, they were actually no more than straggling villages of a hundred or so inhabitants, of importance only to the countryside around them.

The largest and most important of the royal burghs at this time was Edinburgh, but let us look instead at Glasgow, which, though it was a bishop's burgh, nevertheless had all the rights of a royal burgh, for King William the Lion's *charter* had said that he granted to Joseline, Bishop of Glasgow, and to all his successors for ever, '... to have a burgh at Glasgow, with a market ... with all the freedoms and customs which any of my burghs in my whole land ... has'. Some years later he also gave the city the right to have an annual fair for eight days after 6 July, and Glasgow Fair has continued to the present day, though now it is a popular holiday period and has been moved to the last fortnight of July. Let us take an imaginary walk through the Glasgow streets about the year 1510, and this will help to give us a picture of what a burgh was like, at least on the outside.

If we come into Glasgow from the north, we soon see that there is only one main road, called the High Street, which is crossed by two other streets some distance apart. (If you look at the plan on the endpapers, you will be able to see which way we are going.) Long before we even reach the High Street we can see the steeple of the Cathedral, which stands close beside the Molendinar Burn on the spot where St Mungo or Kentigern, the patron saint of Glasgow, built his church in the sixth century. Near by is the

26

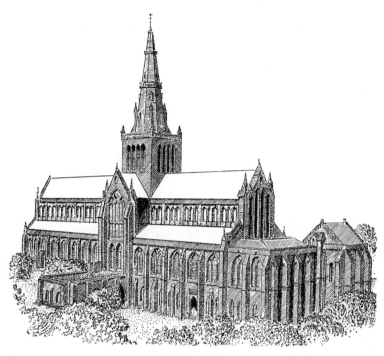

Glasgow Cathedral

bishop's castle. You will be able to think of at least two reasons why the bishop was the most important person in the city, but there was also another one, which was that, in the year 1492, the Pope had ordered that the *see* of Glasgow should become an archbishopric, and that the *dioceses* of Dunblane, Dunkeld, Galloway and Argyll should come under the control of Archbishop Blacader. The present archbishop is called James Beaton, and, if we see him on our walk, we must remember to bow very low to him as we pass.

A little farther on we pass the house of the Provost of the town, the Earl of Lennox, and this, in turn, is not far from St Nicholas Hospital, which is near the corner of Rotten Row and High Street. The street opposite Rotten Row is the Dry Gait, and it gets its name from the fact that it leads to a bridge over the Molendinar, instead of to fords, as the other streets do. As we go on down the High Street we soon come in sight of the College, forerunner of the present University, on the left-hand side of the way. It had been founded in the reign of the present King's grandfather, but the building which we see is the second to be used for this purpose, the first one, known as the 'Auld *Pedagogy*', having been in Rotten Row. Not far from the College is the Grammar School, and from there it is only a short walk to the second pair of cross streets.

If we ask some of the bystanders, they will tell us that the street to the left is the Gallow Gait and that it leads to the Gallowmuir, and that the street ahead of us is called the Walkergait. (By this time you will have guessed that the word 'gait' means street or road.) Following the Walkergait for a short distance, we turn right on to the Briggait, which, as its name tells us, is connected to the north end of the bridge over the Clyde, built by Bishop Rae in the fourteenth century. From the end of the bridge we can see that the Clyde is a very shallow stream – there is a ford farther up – and we can also see the *leper* hospital on the other side, to whose unfortunate inmates King James sometimes gave little gifts, such as in 1497, when he ordered 2*s*. to be given 'to the seke folk at the brig of Glasco'. If the wind is blowing from the east we shall also notice an unpleasant smell coming from the Skinners' Green farther up the river, where wool and skins are laid out to dry, but we can turn quickly up Stockwellgait to St Thenew's Gait, turn right again past the West Port, and arrive back again at the junction of High Street and the Gallowgait.

This is the real centre of the town, for here stands the Cross, where, every Monday, the whole area is busy with people coming and going to the weekly market, housewives and servants keeping a sharp look-out for bargains, stall-holders crying their wares, and friends greeting each other as they pass, each trying to keep to the centre of the road in order to avoid the filth that collects at its sides. Just beside the Cross we can see the building called the *Tolbooth*. The Provost and the councillors, who have been holding a meeting inside, are just coming out and everyone makes way for them respectfully, but, a moment later, they are pressing forward again to see someone hustled through the door, for the Tolbooth is also used as a prison for wrong-doers. Our friends at the

The Canongate Tolbooth, Edinburgh, built 1591

Cross tell us that it is a man who has attacked another and wounded him with his sword during the time of the market – perhaps you can think why people thought this was more serious than an ordinary assault? They also tell us that the

29

old-fashioned weighing-machine which we saw on our way along St Thenew's Gait is the *Tron*, on which all goods bought and sold in the burgh are publicly weighed, and where customs on merchandise are paid. The King gave Bishop Blacader the right to have this Tron in 1490, and that part of St Thenew's Gait where it was placed became known as the Trongait.

Provand's Lordship, Glasgow, built about 1471

From this imaginary tour of the streets of Glasgow we can see that the life of all the burghs must have centred on the area where the Market Cross, the Tolbooth and the Tron stood, and, more often than not, this would be the main street of the town. So far, however, we have not found out what the houses were like, or what it was like to live in a town in the sixteenth century. The picture of the house above tells us a little but let us now see what Don Pedro has to say:

30

'The towns and villages are *populous*. The houses are good, all built of hewn stone and furnished with excellent doors, glass windows and a great number of chimneys. All the furniture that is used in Italy, France and Spain is to be found in their buildings. It has not been bought in modern times only, but inherited from preceding ages. . . .'

Now, how much of this can we believe to be really true? First, we must remember that Don Pedro could not possibly have known all the towns in Scotland, so he is probably writing mostly about Edinburgh. We know that another writer, Alexander Alesius, said in 1529:

'The city itself is not built of brick, but of natural stone squared, so that even the private houses may bear a comparison with great palaces.'

Huntly House, Edinburgh, built in 1570

Let us agree, then, that Don Pedro's description could be true for some of the houses in the capital, but, of course, it would not be true of the other towns in Scotland, such as Aberdeen, in which (we can discover from the records) most of the houses were made of wood. As for the rest of his description, it is true that many houses had glass windows, but they were usually glass above and shutters below, and, though continental furniture was to be found in many dwellings, he does not say how much of it there was. We have already seen that there was very little in the castles, and we can be sure that there would not be any more in the houses of even the well-to-do merchants and *burgesses*, though they did have opportunities in their foreign trade to buy furniture and materials to add to their comfort at home. Here is a list of some of the things a burgess might have in his house, and, as it is taken from a book of laws called LAWS OF THE FOUR BURGHS, we can be pretty sure that it is accurate:

1 trestle-table	2 brewing appliances	1 balance and weights
1 tablecloth	1 kettle	1 chest
1 towel	1 *brander*	1 *girdle*
1 basin	1 *porringer*	1 *platter*
1 laver	1 pitcher	1 crook for pots
1 bed with sheets	1 cauldron	1 pan
1 feather bed	1 form	1 pestle and mortar
1 cup	1 roasting iron	1 bench
1 stool	1 *mazer*[1]	12 spoons

This list is intended to show only what a burgess's house ought to contain, and many burgesses must have owned more. Even so, it makes us realize how very poor the country was in the sixteenth century.

To find out what these Scottish towns were like to live in at this time, we must turn to someone else, someone

[1] See plate facing page 25.

who knew the Edinburgh of James IV at first hand – the poet, William Dunbar. From his two poems, 'To the merchants of Edinburgh' and 'To Aberdeen' we may imagine what the life of the town-dweller was like, and, at first glance, it seems to have been not only unpleasant, but really horrible! Dunbar says:

'May nane pass throw your principal gaittis
For stink of haddockis and scattis,
For cryis of carlingis and debaittis,
For fensum flytingis of defame. . . .'

In present-day English it would be something like this:

'No one can walk through your principal streets
Because of the smell of haddocks and skates,
And the noise of women shouting and scolding,
And the uproar of offensive quarrels. . . .'

If we find this description hard to believe, then we have only to turn to the town records of Edinburgh in James's reign to see that it is really true, and that there were worse things than fishy smells. For example, in February 1490, the provost and council ordered the hangman to fine anyone 4d. who allowed pigs to run loose in the streets and *vennels*, and in 1505, when Thomas Glendinning was appointed to the duty of cleaning the High Street, he was to have a closed cart into which he was to put 'all manner of muck, filth of fish and flesh. . . .' Since there was no regular system of street-cleaning, all the trimmings and odds and ends from the *booths* of the butchers and fish-mongers were flung out on to the street and left there, and the only part of the street which would be reasonably clean was the centre. So everyone wanted to keep to the middle of the road and tried not to give way to anyone else. We can easily guess one cause of the 'debaittis' that Dunbar mentions! These quarrels forced the provost and council

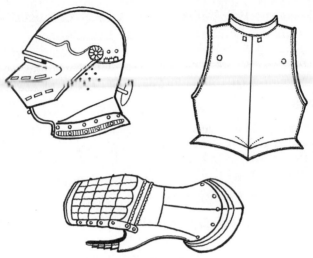

Armour of the sixteenth century

in 1494 to order all merchants and craftsmen to have in their booths at least an axe and a sword, a helmet and *mail gloves*, so that they could help to prevent or break up the fights which often began on the High Street, and which, they said, had led to 'sundrie slaughteris'.

Dunbar's poem goes on as follows:

'Tailyouris, soutteris and craftis vyll
The fairest of your streits dois fyll . . .'

which we could translate by saying that the tailors, shoe-makers and other craftsmen were also responsible for the filthy condition of the principal streets. Cuttings and trimmings were knocked off the skins used by furriers by beating them on the street, and these added to the filth which Thomas Glendinning and his men were expected to clear up; and the smell of the dressed and undressed hides used by the shoemakers and the saddlers only made matters worse.

34

All that we have found out about Edinburgh makes very depressing reading, and we might think it to be scarcely worth while to look at Dunbar's other poem on Aberdeen, in case it shows us an even worse picture. But what a change when we do look! Right away we can see that Dunbar has quite a different story to tell about the northern town. He starts off

'Blyth Aberdeene, thou beriall [beryl] of all tounis
The lamp of bewtie, bountie and blythnes. . . .'

and goes on to say that its reputation for virtue and wisdom has spread everywhere. He wrote this poem when Margaret Tudor, James's queen, was visiting the town in 1511, and he tells us how she was met by the burgesses 'richelie arrayit', that four of them, dressed in velvet gowns, carried a *pall* of crimson velvet above her head as she entered the town and that the artillery fired a salute in her honour. In competition with this there was 'The sound of menstrallis [minstrels] blawing to the sky . . .' (a great contrast to Edinburgh, whose 'commone menstrallis hes no tone') and, after the presentation of a *tableau* there was more music, this time provided by

'. . . four and twentie madinis ying
All claid in greine, of mervelous bewtie,
Playand on timberallis and syngand rycht sweitlie. . . .'

(Twenty-four pretty young girls, all dressed in green frocks, singing sweetly and accompanying themselves on a sort of tambourine.)

Not only had the people gone to a lot of trouble to provide music and what Dunbar calls 'pageants', but apparently the streets were hung with tapestry, and

'At her coming great was the mirth and joy
For at their Cross abundantly ran wine . . .'

35

As before, we must make sure that all this is correct by reading the records of the burgh for the year 1511, and, again, we find that the description is accurate. We see that the provost and the council agreed that Aberdeen must receive the Queen as honourably as any other burgh in Scotland except Edinburgh – which, being the capital, would be expected to put on a better show than any other town. Dwellers on the main street were ordered to hang out 'arres werk' (tapestry) daily 'for the receiving of our sovereign lady, the Queen', and everyone was encouraged with the promise of payment to bring all kinds of greenery, grass and herbs for decorating the town. Unluckily, we are not told how much wine was run at the fountain at the Cross, but, judging by some other entries in the records, it would not be much – and possibly the provost and the councillors would be the first in the queue!

Now, if these were the only entries which we read in the records, we would fall into the trap of believing that Aberdeen was a much nicer place to live in than Edinburgh, at least as far as cleanliness went: so let us look again behind the scenes at some other preparations which had to be made, and they will show us that there was really very little to choose between the two towns, and that Aberdeen, very naturally, was just trying to put on a good show for the Queen. We find that Aberdeen Council had to order that no swine should be allowed to run loose in the streets for the space of fifteen days, on pain of killing the swine and banishing their owners, and that all pigsties were to be removed from the town at once. Second, the *bellman* was to go through the streets and order the removal of all *middens* from the front of the gates and houses, and to announce that anyone who disobeyed would be fined 40s. (How would you like to have to climb over a pile of very nasty refuse when you set off for school each day!) Thus, it is quite clear that Aberdeen, in spite of Dunbar's praise, was very much the same as Edinburgh, and, indeed, the same as every other town in the country in the sixteenth century.

If you have read any other books about life in Britain in the Middle Ages you are sure to have noticed that plagues were very common, though they were not all as serious as the Black Death in the fourteenth century. When we think of what we have found out about the unhealthy conditions in the Scottish towns, we shall not be surprised to find that plague was a frequent visitor in the fifteenth and sixteenth centuries too. The records of the Edinburgh city council can tell us the grim story of one visit of the plague.

March 28, 1498. The provost and council forbid anyone from the parishes of Currie, Under Cramond, Swanston and other parts to come into Edinburgh on the pain of death, because they have received reliable information that these parts are infected by the *pestilence*.

November 17, 1498. It was ordered that no one in the city was to give lodging to anyone from the infected places unless they got special permission from the council, and that a watch was to be set to prevent people from these areas from getting into the city. No one was to be allowed to go to Glasgow without permission, and, if they did, they were to be kept out of the city for forty days after their return. Schools were to be closed, children were forbidden to roam the streets and those children who lived outside Edinburgh were to be sent home.

February 6, 1499. No person was to bring in any wool, skins, hides, cloth or food, or it would be burned at once and the person who brought it in would be banished.

April 27, 1499. The plague was obviously spreading through the whole south-east of Scotland, and the provost

37

and the council, in a desperate endeavour to save Edinburgh, forbade any citizen to give lodging or shelter to people from either Haddington or Kelso, or to go to Peebles without permission.

June 8, 1499. In spite of their precautions the plague must have reached the capital itself, for the orders about schools and children on the streets are repeated. Also, merchants' booths were to be closed, no market was to be held in the town, and anyone having stocks of corn, wine or flour in Leith was to bring it quickly to Edinburgh. If these orders were carried out properly, the usually busy, noisy streets must have become strangely silent, deserted by all except those who had to be out-of-doors on duty or on business, and even they would hurry along, their mouths and noses covered by the ends of their cloaks, afraid to breathe too deeply in case the plague was in the very air, afraid to stop to speak to friends in case one might become infected by the other.

November 27, 1499. Will Rae, George Stewart, James Galloway and Alexander Stobo were appointed to be cleaners and bearers for the city, and were to be paid 1s. a day, '. . . because their labours are heavy and dangerous'. They were indeed dangerous, as these men had to carry away the dead and clean up the infected houses, and their chances of avoiding infection were very small, as the next entry shows.

February 19, 1500. On this date David Hales and four other men were appointed to the same work – the first four must have died of the plague. Hales and his helpers were each to carry a little white wand so that people would know to keep away from them, and they were to be paid a wage of 6d. a day, with extra for cleaning houses and for burying the dead. At the same time, orders were issued that all houses where the plague had been were to be carefully cleaned, and that all goods were to be washed in the running Water of Leith and not in wells, or in the South or North Lochs, for fear of the water supply becoming infected.

Even in the middle of October orders were still being issued about infected houses and the care of the sick, though by that time the plague must have been losing its grip on the city. Thus, this particular visitation had lasted for at least fifteen or sixteen months in a serious form. It was to return again in 1502 and in 1504–5; and it was to make another attack seven years later, on the eve of an even greater disaster for the whole of Scotland.

In the chapter you have just finished you have seen something of the kind of life lived by the people in James IV's reign, and you will be quite right if you feel that it was a hard life and often a dangerous one – very different from the one that we live today. But, at the same time, it was a most interesting period in which to be alive, and in the next chapters we shall hear about some of the happenings of the years 1488–1513 and try to see in what ways they were important for the future of Scotland.

A New Kind of King

James IV lived at a time when, in various countries in Europe – in England, France and Italy, for instance – kings and princes were beginning to be interested in new things and to want a new kind of servant to help them to carry out their plans. The nobles were in many ways conservative, that is, old-fashioned, and did not understand or like these new ideas. They were much better at fighting than anything else, and could not see why a king should be interested in new discoveries of science and geography, in new ways of government, in education or in poetry. Above all, they disliked the new way of government through servants who were not nobles, though they might be very clever.

This was one of the reasons why the nobles were discontented under James III, whose favourites included a tailor, a shoemaker, a fencing master, a musician and an architect called Robert Cochrane, the man who may have designed the Great Hall of Stirling Castle and whom the King had created the Earl of Mar. The nobles believed that these favourites gave the King bad advice about the government of the country, and in 1482 they got rid of them by hanging them over the bridge at Lauder in the presence of the King himself. You can read the whole story and see how the Earl of Angus got his nickname 'Bell-the-Cat' in Sir Walter Scott's TALES OF A GRANDFATHER.

James IV in many ways liked the same things as his father. He, too, was interested in all the things which

The Palace of Holyroodhouse, with the James IV Tower on the left

King's College Chapel, Aberdeen. The College was founded in 1495

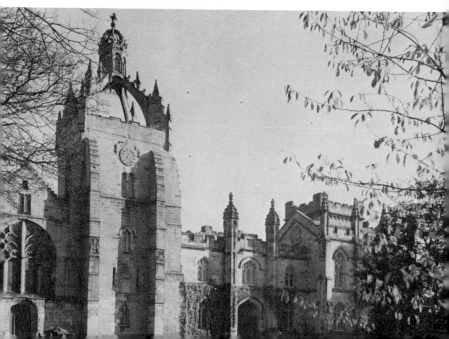

Bishop Elphinstone of Aberdeen, who played a big part in the founding of the University

King Henry VII of England, father-in-law of James IV

The Great Hall, Stirling Castle, as it is today

excited the inventors, explorers, scholars, builders and artists of the time, and there were many of these in Europe, for this was an exciting time of new discoveries which we call the Renaissance. Renaissance means re-birth. We call James a Renaissance king because he shared in the interests which were re-born at this time. We will now find out what he did – together with his friends and servants – to bring these new ideas to Scotland.

EDUCATION AND LEARNING

How many times have you wished that you did not have to go to school, or, that you could do something to prevent it from opening? – like the boy who lived on Tweedside in

the twelfth century, who disliked school so much that he
threw the key of the school building into the river! But
present-day schools are so much nicer than they used to
be, with more subjects to learn and pleasant buildings to
work in, whereas schools in James IV's reign were often
just a single room in a private house, and the subjects
were usually Latin, reading and writing. If you had gone
to school in Aberdeen in the middle of the sixteenth century, for example, you would not have been allowed to
speak English, even to your friends, for pupils were forbidden to speak any language but Latin, Hebrew, Greek,
French or Gaelic!

In James's reign there was probably a school of some
kind in every large town in Scotland. Many of them were
connected with the Church and most of the pupils in
them intended to become clergymen when they grew up,
so we find that there were schools in monasteries and connected to cathedrals and abbeys, but the most unusual
kind was the 'sang schule', where boys were taught to
sing various kinds of church music, such as *plainsong* and
Gregorian chant, as well as reading, writing and perhaps
some Latin. Can you think why there were special schools
for this? Of course, there were also grammar schools in
the burghs which were under the control of the Council,
but the Church played a very big part in education at this
time, and it is not surprising that Scotland's first three
universities were all founded by bishops.

Most of you will know that today everyone must go to
school because an Act of Parliament says so. Some of you
may even know that the first Act which made education
compulsory for all Scottish children over the age of five
was passed in 1872: but not so many will have heard about
still another 'Education Act' which was passed by Parliament nearly five hundred years ago, in the year 1496.

This is what it says:

> 'It is *statute* and *ordained* . . . that all barons and freeholders . . . put
> their eldest sons and heirs to the schools from the time they be six or
> nine years of age and to remain at the grammar schools till they . . . have
> perfect Latin: and thereafter to remain three years at the schools of
> art and law, so that they may have knowledge and understanding of
> the laws . . . so that they that are *Sheriffs* or Judges . . . may have
> knowledge to do justice. . . .'

Thus we can see that both the King and the Parliament
were eager to improve the education of at least some of the
people, so that, in turn, they could help to improve the
government of the country. But there was one drawback
to this plan – neither St Andrews nor Glasgow Universities had classes in civil law, and anyone who wanted to
become a lawyer had to go to either Paris or Orleans to
study. No one knew this better than Bishop Elphinstone[1]
of Aberdeen, for he himself had studied at Glasgow before
going to Paris, first as a student and then as a teacher, and,
though we do not know for sure, most probably he suggested to James that it would be a good idea to found a
university at Aberdeen. The King wrote to Pope Alexander VI, who, in February 1495, gave James permission
to carry out his plan – because, as the Pope's *Bull* said,
'. . . in the northerly parts of the kingdom there are some
places separated from the rest of the realm by arms of the
sea and very steep mountains, in which regions dwell men
who are uncultivated and ignorant of letters.'

Bishop Elphinstone now got busy. He saw that tools and
gunpowder were imported from the Continent to help
with the buildings: he arranged that the new university
should have enough money to pay the teachers and also to
pay for the teaching of some poor scholars; he appointed
Hector Boece, the Scottish historian, as the first Principal,

[1] See plate facing page 41.

43

and arranged that there should be classes in *theology*, church law and civil law, medicine and the arts; and, not content with this, in 1505 he also founded St Mary's College, which soon afterwards became known as King's College, as it still is.[1]

Though the foundation of Aberdeen University was the most important improvement in education in James's reign, there were others almost as great. Curiously enough, though Scotland now had three universities, James sent his son Alexander to study in Padua in Italy – can you guess why? – and the great scholar Erasmus was engaged to tutor the young man. Perhaps you would be interested to know what he studied. In the mornings he worked at *rhetoric* and Greek, and each afternoon he played on the

[1] See plate facing page 40.

Erasmus, the great Dutch scholar

monochord, flute or lute, sometimes singing to his own accompaniment. Even at meal-times someone read aloud to those who were present, and discussions might take place; if there was any time left, Alexander studied history, which he liked very much. While still very young he had been made Archbishop of St Andrews, and he was also Chancellor of the University. When he returned to Scotland he was horrified to find that, owing to a lack of good teachers and to a lack of money, the University was in a very bad state indeed. There was already one college, called St Salvator's, founded by Bishop Kennedy, and, to try to improve matters, Alexander and Prior John Hepburn founded the College of St Leonard in 1512, in which twenty students of arts and six of theology were to be educated.

Now, so far it would seem that much of the praise for the improvements in education should go to Bishop Elphinstone and to the King's son, but there are at least two more things which James himself helped to do: the founding of the College of Surgeons and the introduction of printing.

You remember that, in the first chapter, we learned about the wild doings of the Abbot of Unreason? Well, in 1504 there is a strange little entry in the Treasurer's Accounts which says:

To a barber who healed Paul's head when he was hurt by the Abbot of Unreason ... 14*s.*

It seems very odd to us that it was a barber who was called in to help Paul, and not a doctor, as it would be today, but at this time surgeons and barbers belonged to the same *craft*. In 1505 the Council of Edinburgh agreed to a request from the surgeons and barbers of the town that anyone wishing to practise these arts must first of all pass an examination in *anatomy*; that they were to be given the body of an executed criminal once a year on which to practise anatomy; that apprentices must be able to read and write; and that the entry fee was to be £5 and a dinner to all the masters of the craft. As we shall see farther on, James himself was interested in the work of a doctor, and, perhaps because of this, he confirmed the grant the next year and the College of Surgeons was started.

The Royal College of Surgeons as it is now

Until the beginning of the sixteenth century students at the Scottish universities had to depend on printed books which were imported from England or Europe for their studies. As you can guess, this was very awkward – think how annoying it would be to have to write to Oxford or Paris for any book that you wanted, especially when there were no regular train or boat services or post offices, as there are now. In 1507, therefore, James gave permission to Walter Chepman and Andrew Myllar to set up a press in the Cowgate of Edinburgh to print law books, Acts of Parliament, religious books and chronicles; at the same time, he forbade people to have manuscripts printed anywhere else, so that the two men would be able to make a profit from their work. The first printing which was done from this press was Bishop Elphinstone's ABERDEEN BREVIARY, some popular tales and ballads, and an edition of Blind Harry's poem 'Wallace'.

Myller's printing device

Quhais poᵂer ᵂiſedome ꝛ honoure
Js infynite ſalbe ꝛ eᵂir ᵂas ᵂes
As in the principall mencioñ of the meſſe
All thir ſayd thingis reforñ as thou beſt thinkis
Quhilk ar degradit foꝛ pure pitee redꝛeſſe
Sen ᵂant of ᵂiſe makis ſit in binkis

Part of a poem by Henryson, printed by Chepman and Myller

Thus, the most important invention of this time and the one which did most to spread learning and knowledge in every civilized country was brought into Scotland by the express command of the King himself.

But James was not content just to order improvements to be made – he was eager to try things out for himself. We would say today that the King was very interested in scientific research, and he would certainly have enjoyed working with some of the scientific kits which you can buy today in any toyshop. But in the sixteenth century these were not thought of, and James studied what was called alchemy. He was very eager to discover the 'quinta essencia', which means fifth essence and from which we get our word 'quintessence'. It was a liquid which was supposed to have the power of turning other metals into gold and of making people live longer. It is easy for us to laugh at this idea, but we must remember that a great many other people firmly believed that this liquid could be found and spent much of their time in trying to find it, and also, that this study of alchemy was the forerunner of the modern chemistry which you learn in school.

James tried other experiments too. There is a tale that he had two young children put in charge of a dumb woman on an island to see what language they would speak when they were old enough, but this story is not likely to be true. But there is no doubt about his interest in dentistry and surgery, for in 1511 the Treasurer twice paid out 14s. to people from whom the King had extracted teeth – how nice if our dentists paid us to have our teeth attended to, instead of the other way about! – and another time he paid 2s. 8d. for bandages for 'John Barbour's sore leg, which the King healed'.

The person who helped James most in his search for the 'quinta essencia' was a man called John Damien, whom the King made Abbot of Tungland as a reward for his services. Furnaces for his experiments were set up in Edinburgh and Stirling, and a lot of money was spent on such things as bellows, glass flasks, *mortars*, *crucibles*, charcoal, quicksilver, *aqua vitae*, salt, eggs and drugs of many kinds. Of course, he was not successful, but one of his experiments has become famous. This was the attempt that he made, in 1507, to fly from the battlements of Stirling Castle with the help of a pair of wings made out

Stirling Castle

of feathers. As you can imagine, the Abbot did not fly far. He landed at the foot of the Castle rock, and was lucky to escape with only a broken leg and not a broken neck! His excuse for his failure was that his wings were made of hens' feathers, and, as everyone knows, hens do not like to fly far from the ground – but we do not hear of him trying again with a different pair of wings! Dunbar wrote a poem about it; we shall see a verse of it later on.

GOVERNMENT

We started off this chapter by finding out about the trouble which James III had with his barons and how this led to civil war, but have you noticed that there does not seem to be much of this trouble in James IV's reign? James did have revolts to deal with, but, generally speaking, the nobles were peaceful while he was on the throne.

Probably the most important reason was that James himself was a much more likeable person than his father, and, though he resembled him in encouraging learning and in enjoying the company of clever people, he also excelled in games and athletic feats, and especially in horsemanship. He could leap on to his horse without using the stirrups, and ride more than one hundred miles in a day; we shall also see that he was eager to become skilful in shooting, both with the *hand culverin* and with bows and arrows. Thus, those barons who did not think much of book learning probably felt that he was as good as they were in the things which they did admire.

The two parts of the kingdom which gave the King most trouble were the Highlands and the Borders, because they were far away and difficult to get at, but this did not stop James. He was in the Highlands or Islands six times in the first seven years of his reign, and, finally, because of the trouble that he was causing, the King abolished the title of Lord of the Isles, and gave control of the northern area to the Earl of Huntly and the Earl of Argyll. He also tried to make friends with the Highland chiefs, and he must have been successful in doing so, as a large number fought for him at Flodden. He also visited the Borders on many occasions, accompanying his officials on their '*justice-ayres*' to help them to crush the lawlessness which was so common. This is how a visit of the King to Jedburgh in 1510 was described, changed into modern English:

'The King rode forth from Edinburgh on the 8th of November . . . to the Water of Rule where he captured various *broken men* and brought them to Jedburgh, of whom some were executed: and the leaders of the trouble-makers came dressed in linen clothes . . . with ropes round their necks and threw themselves on the King's mercy, who sent them as prisoners to various castles . . . after which the Borders were very much quieter.'

By taking this firm line in both the Highlands and the Borders James was able to make sure that Scotland was a more peaceful place to live in than it had been for a long time. As Don Pedro said, 'None of the former kings have succeeded in bringing the people into such *subjection* as the present king.'

Finally, James set up a new court in Edinburgh called the 'Daily Council' to do some of the work which the other courts did not have time for, and especially to help poor people, whose complaints were sometimes put off for year after year. Thus, it is clear that James was keenly interested in the work of keeping the country orderly and peaceful and in giving her a good and firm government, rather in the way that his father-in-law Henry VII[1] was doing in England at the same time.

There is one last thing which James did that helped a little in the task of governing the country, but it deserves a section all to itself.

ARTILLERY

In the spring of the year 1511 a small group of men strolled along the water-front of the port of Dieppe in France, to look at the ship in which they were to travel to Scotland. We know the names of four of them – there were Gervase, the gunner, John Garnere, Steven Davennais and Jacat of Tours, who were *melters*, and several others, including a carpenter and a blacksmith. No doubt, as they went on board, they chatted about the new country which they were to see for the first time; possibly they complained about the time that they had wasted in Dieppe, first waiting for the ship, and then for a fair wind for Scotland, for this delay had cost them £35 0s. 3d. for board and lodging. Luckily, they were not out of pocket, as the money had been paid by the King's agent in Dieppe,

[1] See plate facing page 41.

for these men were badly wanted by James, both to make guns and also to show others how to do so.

Three years before this the King had become very keen about shooting, and had bought at least five hand-culverins for his own use, which had cost him £37 16s. Guns of this period were of two kinds. There were cannons of large *calibre*, called *bombards* or sometimes 'murderers', which were used for sieges, and smaller ones, called

Mons Meg

culverins or *serpentines*, which could be carried on carts when the army marched. Probably the most famous gun in Scotland even today is Mons Meg, and those of you who have seen it at Edinburgh Castle will know roughly what the guns in James's artillery looked like, though, of course, Mons Meg is much bigger than any made at this time. It is constructed of long flat bars of metal held together with hoops, but at this time the *casting* of guns was begun, and that is why James needed skilled men from France and Flanders, as they understood how to do this properly.

In 1508, the year in which James became interested in shooting, the manufacture of guns began at Stirling and Edinburgh, and after 1511 gun-making on a big scale

Edinburgh Castle

began at Edinburgh Castle. Large quantities of iron and other metals were brought from the Continent for the foreign workers to use, and thousands of cannon balls of different sizes were also imported, while at home squads of workmen made ammunition wagons, wooden carriages for the guns, gunpowder, *handspikes*, spades and shovels for levelling the ground in front of the guns when they moved, and harness for the oxen that pulled them along. All through 1511 and 1512 this work went on under the watchful eye of Robert Borthwick, whom we shall meet again at the end of this story in charge of the guns that he had helped to make.

As we shall see in the next chapter, James specially wanted to have a large, powerful navy, and, of course, he needed a lot of guns for the ships that were being built. At the same time, when the nobles learned that James had a number of cannon which could make short work of their castles, it made them think twice about rebelling against the King, and this helped to keep the country peaceful.

A sixteenth-century gun

53

If someone were to ask you for the name of a great English poet before the days of Shakespeare, you would probably think at once of Chaucer, who wrote the famous CANTER-BURY TALES, one of the *classics* of English literature. His work was very much admired by the poets of James IV's reign also, and they even tried to imitate his style and often said that they were sorry that they could not write as well as he had done.

There were five well-known poets (or *Makars*, as they were called) who were alive between 1488 and 1513, when James was on the throne. The first was Robert Henryson, a schoolmaster of Dunfermline, who, in addition to some longer poems, turned some of Aesop's FABLES into Scots verse. The best is 'The Tale of the Country Mouse and the Town Mouse', in which the town mouse invites her sister from the country for a visit, promising her better food and a more comfortable house than she was accustomed to. But, says Henryson:

> 'Eftir joye ofttymes cummis care
> And truble eftir gret prosperite.
> Thus as thai sat in all thair jolyte
> So come the spensar with keyis intill hand
> Opinnit the dure and thaim at dynere fand.'

In modern English that verse might be something like this:

> 'After joy ofttimes comes care
> And trouble after great prosperity.
> Thus, as they sat in greatest jollity
> The pantryman appeared, with keys in hand,
> Opened the door and them at dinner found.'

The country mouse was terrified that she should be caught, and, no sooner had she recovered from this shock than Gilbert, the cat, appeared, and it was only by luck that she escaped being eaten. After this second terrifying experience the country mouse left immediately for her own home, and the *moral* of the fable, the poet says, is:

> 'Blissit be sympill lyf withoutin dreid;
> Blissit be sobir feist and quiete:
> Quha has eneugh, of no mor has he neid
> Thocht it be littill into quantite.'

Or, as we might say:

> 'Blest is the simple life that knows no fear;
> Blest are the meals that one consumes in peace:
> For, if we have enough, we need no more,
> Although it may be small in quantity.'

Three of the other four poets of the reign were Gavin Douglas, third son of 'Bell-the-Cat', who translated Virgil's AENEID into verse, Blind Harry, who is thought to have been the author of a poem about the deeds of Sir William Wallace, and Sir David Lindsay, but his great play in verse A SATIRE OF THE THREE ESTATES, was not written till after James's death.

The last is William Dunbar, whose poetry we have already read (pages 33–35). He was born about 1460 and went to St Andrew's University, where he took his degree. After that, we do not know much about him. He was probably a wandering scholar for a time in England and France before he returned to James's court, where he was given a job, possibly as a clerk. Later, he became a priest, and James granted him a pension of £80 a year, which was more than twice as much as the Principal of Aberdeen University earned. There is no doubt that he is among the finest of the Scottish poets, but his poetry is sometimes difficult for us to understand, as the language has changed so much since Dunbar wrote. Here is a good hint: find the

Sir David Lindsay's coat of arms

meanings of the words that you don't know, and then read the poems aloud, and you will find that they are much easier than they look. But, if you should still have difficulty, there is an English version below each piece which will give you a lot of help. We will start with a part of something that you already know about – the Abbot of Tungland's attempted flight:

'. . . he assailyeit,
To mak the quintessance, and failyeit;
And quhen he saw that nocht availyeit,
A *fedrem* on he tuke,   (plumage; wings)
And *schupe* in Turky for to fle;   (undertook)

And quhen that he did mont on he,
All fowill *ferleit* quhat he sowld be,   (wondered)
That evir did on him luke.
And evir the cuschettis at him tuggit,
The rukis him rent, the ravynis him druggit,
The hudit crawis his hair furth ruggit,
The hevin he micht not bruke.
He *schewre* his feddreme that was schene,   (tore off)
And slippit owt of it full clene,
And in a myre, up to the ene,
Amang the glar did glyd.'

Here is the English version:

'. . . he tried
To make the quintessence, and failed,
And when he saw his plans go wrong
He then prepared a pair of wings,
To fly to Turkey – so he said!
When he had risen from the ground
The birds that saw him in the sky
Began to wonder what he was.
At once the pigeons tugged at him,
The rooks and ravens tore and dragged,
The hooded crows pulled out his hair,
He could no longer stay on high.
He shed his shining plumage then:
Free from his home-made wings he fell;
And in a marsh, up to the eyes,
He slid among the mud!'

As you can guess from these lines, Dunbar did not like
the Abbot, as the latter was an *impostor* and yet had been
given a high position in the Church; while Dunbar, who
was a great poet, had got very little. This is what he thinks
of the matter:

'I knaw nocht how the kirk is gydit
Bot *benefices* are nocht leill devydit;
Sum men hes sevin, and I nocht ane:
Quhilk to considder is ane pane.'

.   .   .

> 'I can't think how the Church is ruled
> For *livings* are not fairly shared;
> Some men have seven, and I not one;
> To think of this gives me a pain!'

One of the things that makes Dunbar's poems so interesting is that he can write well about almost anything at all. He has poems on a headache and on a dance in the Queen's rooms; he has a 'flyting' (scolding) with a fellow poet called Walter Kennedy; a poem on an imaginary fight between the tailors and the shoemakers, and a famous one on the marriage of James IV and Margaret Tudor, called 'The Thistle and the Rose', as well as *allegories* and *petitions* and many others of different kinds – over eighty at least, and perhaps more. One of the most famous is 'The Dance of the Seven Deadly Sins', in which Dunbar describes how, while dreaming, he saw this entertainment which had been ordered by the Devil for his own amusement. This is the last verse:

> 'Than cryd Mahoun for a Heland padyane;
> Syne ran a feynd to feche Makfadyane,
> Far northwart in a nuke:
> Be he the correnoch had done schout,
> Erschemen so gadderit him abowt,
> In Hell grit rowme they tuke.
> Thae tarmegantis, with tag and tatter,
> Full lowd in Ersche begowth to clatter,
> And rowp lyk revin and ruke:
> The Devill sa devit wes with thair yell,
> That in the depest pot of Hell
> He smorit thame with smuke.'

The English version could be as follows:

> 'Then called the De'il for a Highland pageant;
> A fiend ran off to fetch MacFadyen,
> Far northward in a nook:
> When he the coronach had played,

58

Highlanders crowded all around,
In Hell great room they took:
These boisterous folk in tattered clothes,
In Gaelic now began to chatter,
And croak like raven and rook.
The De'il was deafened with their din,
And in the deepest pit of Hell
He smothered them with smoke.'

What did James think of all the writing that was being done in his reign? Unluckily, we do not know, and Don Pedro probably exaggerates a bit when he says that the King was well read. At least he must have enjoyed hearing Dunbar's poems read or recited at court on winter evenings, otherwise he would not have given him such a large pension, but he could not possibly guess that he was listening to poetry which would still be read and enjoyed by people nearly five hundred years afterwards.

NEW BUILDINGS

James was probably more interested in buildings and architecture than in literature, and the Treasurer must often have lain awake at night worrying where to get the money for the King's latest projects. The new Palace of Holyroodhouse[1] was begun before the arrival of Queen Margaret, and another at Faulkland, which was intended to be used as a hunting lodge. It had fishponds and an enclosure for deer, and provided such things as swans and wild boars for the meals of the King and his guests at Holyroodhouse. Improvements and additions were made at Stirling Castle and to various other fortresses such as those at Dingwall, Inverness, Lochmaben, Tarbert and Dunbar; and the south side was added to the Palace of Linlithgow. In this liking for building James resembled

[1] See plate facing p. 40.

Falkland Palace, Fife. A later picture

his unfortunate father, and, indeed, many other kings in
Europe at this time. These rulers loved magnificence in
their palaces and wanted to be remembered for the fine
buildings they left behind them.

So in many ways James was a Renaissance king, interested in education, better government and some of the new and exciting ideas which were being talked over and tried out in many countries of Europe at this time.

Trade and the Scottish Navy

Very early on a summer morning in the year 1490 two ships flying the Scottish flag came sailing into the Firth of Forth. One was the 'Yellow Carvel', commanded by Sir Andrew Wood, and the other was the 'Flower'. As the light increased, their sailors cheerfully went about their tasks of preparing the ships for harbour, pleased to be back safe after their voyage to Flanders, and looking forward to seeing their friends and relatives again. Suddenly, they became aware that three ships were appearing from behind the Isle of May, and, as they approached, they could see that they were flying the St George's Cross of England and that they were preparing for battle. We will let the old historian, Robert Lindsay of Pitscottie, tell the rest of the story, but in modern English and changed a little to make it easier to understand.

'Sir Andrew Wood, seeing this, urged his men to prepare for battle, saying, "Set yourselves in order. Let the gunners load their artillery, let the *crossbowmen* make ready, with the *lime-pots* and the *fire-balls* in our *tops* and the men with the two-handed swords in the *forecastle*. And let every man be strong and diligent for the honour of this realm."

'The sun began to rise and shine on the sails, and the English appeared very

A Crossbowman

frightful to the Scots, for their ships were big and strong and well supplied with big guns which they fired at the Scots ships. But the Scots closed with the English and they fought in this position all the long summer day, from sunrise to sunset, while all the people who lived near the coast came down to the shore to watch. The next morning the trumpets were sounded and the ships closed and fought so desperately that the crews scarcely noticed that the tide and a south wind had drifted them, still fighting, to the mouth of the Tay, where, at length, the English commander, Stephen Bull, surrendered, and his ships were towed into the town of Dundee. Sir Andrew Wood handed over his prisoners to the King, who gave them gifts of gold and silver and returned their ships, and sent them back to the King of England, to let him understand that he had as good men, both by sea and land, in Scotland as in England.'

Though nothing important has been left out of that little story, it does leave us with one or two questions to which we would like answers. Why did the English ships attack the Scots in peacetime; who was their commander, Stephen Bull; and, especially interesting, who was Sir Andrew Wood? To find out some of the answers we must go back to the previous year, when five English ships had appeared in the Forth and had attacked and plundered Scottish shipping. The King and Council had asked several captains if they would try to drive off these pirates, but they could get no one to volunteer until they asked Sir Andrew Wood, who, with his two ships attacked the English five and forced them to surrender. King Henry of England was furious, and is believed to have offered a reward for Sir Andrew, dead or alive. Stephen Bull agreed to try to win it – and we know the result.

Sir Andrew himself was a merchant of Leith, but he had been given an estate at Largo in Fife for faithful service to James III – you remember, it was to Sir Andrew's ships that James was fleeing when he was killed. Now, as we have seen, he was one of James IV's best captains, equally ready to sail out against heavy odds with the two royal ships or to hire them from the King and go off on a peaceful trading voyage to the Continent. These ships were what we would call armed merchantmen, and were let out for trading purposes in peacetime at a certain amount for each voyage – for example, the 'Douglas' was hired for £45 by James Wood in 1496, and the 'Christopher' by John Irvine for £100 for the whole year.

In the time of James IV Scotland traded with France, the Baltic lands, England and Ireland, but most of her trade was carried on with Flanders, and it was supposed to pass through certain *staple ports*. These ports had the *monopoly* of handling all the trade, and, in return, they gave the merchants certain rights. At this time, the staple port in the Netherlands was first at Bruges, then Middel-

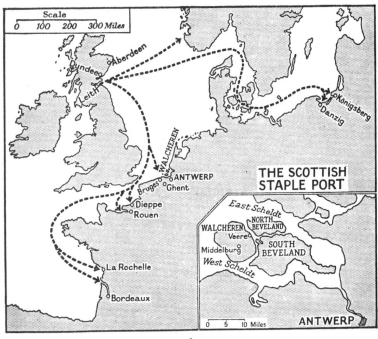

An old picture of Veere

burg and finally at Veere. (Can you find these places on the map?) The rights of the Scottish merchants at these ports were looked after by a person called the Conservator, and the first one that we know to have held that position was a man called Andrew Halyburton, from whose ledger for the years 1492–1503 we can learn a great deal about the trade that was carried on between the two countries. The reason why Scotland traded so much with Flanders was that the latter was a great cloth-producing country and Scotland could sell her the wool from the large flocks of sheep which she raised. Also, her other exports could be sold in the markets of the great trading cities of Antwerp, Ghent and Bruges, where, as early as 1291, there was a street called 'Scotland'. We have already seen in the first chapter that the country did not have much to sell, and, apart from wool, there were only skins of various kinds, especially marten skins, the finest to be had anywhere; the hides of cattle; some badly made cloth; salted fish and large pearls, though these were not so fine or so valuable as those of the East. The fish were mainly salmon and herring, and we can tell that this was quite an important export because the customs duties paid on them at the end of James III's reign were £700, or about a quarter of the duties paid on wool and hides. To make people try to catch more fish, Parliament passed an Act in 1493 ordering that fishing boats of at least twenty tons should be built at all the main ports of Scotland, and that any idle men should be employed in them as seamen. This seems to us to be a good idea, but when we find that that Act had to be repeated in 1503 we can guess that it was not very successful.

Though Scotland did not have very much to export she

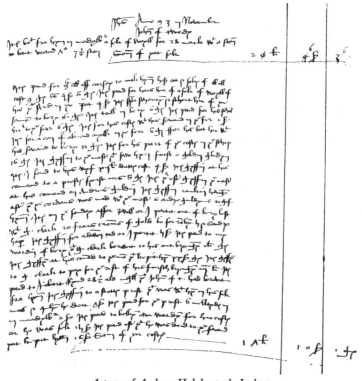

A page of Andrew Halyburton's Ledger

had to buy a great deal from abroad, for she was not a manufacturing country. So, to give us an idea of the things that were imported in James's reign, let us pick out some entries from Andrew Halyburton's ledger. We will turn them into present-day English to make them easier to read.

SENT TO THE ARCHBISHOP OF ST. ANDREWS

Books	500 gold crowns		
A tomb, bought in Bruges	£22	0	0

SENT TO JANET PATERSON

34½ *ells* of velvet	£17	5	0
2 pieces of *fustian*	1	4	0
3 pieces of *chequered cloth*	2	11	0
50 lb of almonds		12	6
50 lb of rice		7	0
17 lb of pepper		19	0
1 roll canvas		7	0

SENT TO SIR ROBERT WELLS IN THE 'FLOWER'

A Spanish sword	£	19	6
A little tin of ginger		7	6
Half a ream of paper		1	6
A bag		4	4
2 *vestments* for priests	2	7	0
An altar-hanging		13	0
A piece of *lawn*	2	8	0

SENT TO THE ABBOT OF HOLYROOD

3 *puncheons* of wine	7	17	0
2 barrels of apples		11	6
2 lb of *saffron*	1	0	0
25 cases of sugar		8	2
12 lb confectionery		5	0
drugs		10	8

SENT TO THE DUKE OF ROSS (THE KING'S BROTHER)

125 ells of linen cloth	£3	2	6
4 feather beds	4	0	0
4 other beds	3	8	0
12 pillows	1	4	0
12 candlesticks		13	4
3 doz. pewter dishes and 3 chargers	9	14	9
1 doz. table napkins		9	0
1 doz. cushions		16	0
2 *chandeliers*	1	7	0
7 ells brown cloth	2	12	6
6 ells black satin	2	8	0
3 ells crimson satin	2	11	0

SENT TO THE BISHOP OF ABERDEEN

1 barrel gunpowder	£4	16	4
Carts and wheelbarrows	4	1	0
2 silver *chalices*	13	0	5
1 piece black cloth	9	0	0
2 black bonnets		6	0
2 red caps		7	0
1 repaired clock and a case for it.		3	0

From these entries we can see quite easily that almost everything except just the bare necessities of life had to be imported into Scotland – spices, wine, fruit, paper, sugar, furnishings, dishes, drugs and silverware, not counting Bishop Elphinstone's gunpowder and wheelbarrows for the building of Aberdeen University; but the import of fine cloth outweighed all others. No wonder Parliament had to pass Acts forbidding anyone but knights and nobles to wear costly clothes! About the only things which are not mentioned in the above lists are the iron, wood and naval stores of all kinds which were needed for the building of a navy, and which came mainly from France and from the countries round the Baltic Sea.

To us, in these days of space travel, a voyage to France or Flanders does not seem to be anything to get excited

Scottish coins of James IV's reign

about, but, as we have seen, it was looked on as a 'wild adventure' in James's day. The ships themselves were very small and a law was passed in the reign of James's father forbidding them to sail from the end of October until the beginning of February, for fear of storms. In addition, the captains had no accurate charts, but the biggest danger was from attack by the vessels of other countries, whether there was a war going on or not. The Scots ships often suffered from attacks from English, Dutch and Portuguese pirates; but, of course, the Scots skippers were not always innocent themselves!

As well as Sir Andrew Wood, James had three other famous captains, John, Robert and Andrew Barton. Many years before, their father's ship had been attacked by some Portuguese vessels, and the King of Portugal had refused to give him any *compensation*. The brothers therefore got permission from James to attack Portuguese ships in revenge, but we can be pretty sure that Andrew at least used this as an excuse to attack the ships of other nations and to steal their goods. In 1511 some English merchants complained to King Henry VIII, who sent out the Admiral of England, Sir Edward Howard, and his brother Lord Thomas. The latter, while lying in the Downs, spotted Andrew Barton with the 'Lion' and the 'Jenny Pirwin' and immediately attacked. The Scots fought furiously, returning the fire of the English and beating off all attacks, but eventually their captain was mortally wounded:

> 'Fight on, my men,' said Sir Andrew Barton,
> 'I am a little hurt, but I am not slain.
> I'll lay me down to bleed awhile,
> And then I'll rise to fight again.'

At last the English sailors could no longer hear the whistle which he blew to encourage his men, and they boarded the two ships and made the crews prisoner. King Henry sent them back to Scotland and refused to punish the Howards as James demanded – but we shall see later that this was not the end of the matter.

Now we must look at the navy about which James was so keen. Why did the King, the first to take a real interest in the navy since the days of Robert Bruce, spend so much money on shipbuilding when Scotland was such a poor country? Well, you can think of at least one answer to that question, and perhaps two – to help to protect Scottish trade, and because all the other countries on the Atlantic sea-board were becoming very interested in sea exploration at this time. In 1486 Bartholomew Diaz sailed round the Cape of Good Hope; Columbus discovered the West Indies in 1492; and in 1497 Vasco da

Gama sailed to India and John Cabot to the coast of America. But the third and most important reason was that James dreamed of leading another Crusade to the East, to conquer the heathen Turks and get back Jerusalem. For such a venture a fleet was a necessity. It seems strange to think of a crusade against the Turks in the sixteenth century, but James was not the only ruler to talk about it, though he was probably the only one who really believed that it could be carried out. It may have been to show that he was in earnest about it that he sent Robert Barton to offer a silver ship weighing $31\frac{1}{2}$ oz. at the shrine of St James of Compostella in Spain, who had been the patron saint of an order of knights during the Crusades.

As a result, we find men journeying from Scotland to almost every country on the sea-coast of Europe, and returning with loads of timber, iron, pulleys, cordage, masts, anchors and canvas. Skilled carpenters – John Lawrence, Jeannen Diew and Jacat Terrell – were brought from France; a new port, dockyard and ropeworks were constructed at Newhaven, and docks were also built at Airth, near Stirling, where ships could be taken for repairs or refitting. This worked rather like the modern dry-dock – the ship was placed inside, the end of the dock was closed with clay and the water was scooped out. When the repairs were finished the clay was removed and the ship was floated out again, sometimes with the help of empty barrels which were lashed to her sides so as to raise her in the water.

Unluckily, it is very difficult to say exactly how many ships James had, what size they were or even how much they cost to build, though it is possible that he was spending as much as £15,000 a year on the navy alone – a huge sum for such a poor country. We can get an idea of the number of ships by reading a letter written by Lord

Dacre to Henry VIII in 1513 telling him of the preparations for war which were then being made in Scotland, in which he says that at Leith there were thirteen big ships of three tops, ten small ships and an English ship captured by one of James's captains, and at Newhaven there were two more big ones under repair, the 'James' and the 'Margaret'. If we can believe these figures to be true, then James had a really strong navy, though, of course, they were not all constructed in the royal dockyards – there would not have been enough time or wood to build all these, and, in any case, we know that at least seven were bought from different people at home and abroad. We also know the names of some of the other Scottish ships as well as the two mentioned above – there was the 'Douglas', 'Eagle', 'Trinity', 'Christopher', 'Lark', 'Pansy', 'Raven', 'Gabriel', 'Unicorn', 'Jacat', 'Colomb', and the 'Treasurer', possibly named after the unfortunate man who had to produce all the money for the shipbuilding! But the largest and the best-known was the 'Great Michael', which was launched about 1511.

She was believed to be the biggest ship in the world at the time, and our old friend Lindsay of Pitscottie says that the total cost of building her was £30,000, not counting the cannon that she carried. He also says that she was 240 ft. long, that her breadth inside was 36 ft. and that her sides were 10 ft. thick. Though they may not have really been as much as this, it does seem that they were unusually thick, for the muzzles of her guns did not stick out beyond them, and the sides of the *gun-ports* had to be covered with leather in case the wood caught fire when the guns were fired. She is supposed to have had six big guns on each side, two big ones at her stern and one at her bow, as well as three hundred pieces of smaller artillery – *falcons, slings, serpentines, hackbutts* and crossbows – 120

The 'Great Michael'

gunners and 300 sailors. Naturally, James was very interested in his great ship and visited her often, sometimes giving the workmen little presents of what was called 'drinksilver', and always remembering to console any who were injured while working on her with gifts of money. The actual launching must have been a thrilling moment for the King and for all who had been building her. Three trumpeters and a drummer were given a total of 17s. between them for playing at the ceremony. Afterwards, when the ship was afloat, we are told that the King ordered a cannon to be fired at her as a test of her strength, and it was said that it did her no harm. If you live in Edinburgh or go there on holiday, you should visit the Royal Scottish

Museum, where you can see models of both the 'Yellow Carvel' and the 'Great Michael'. These will give you a very good idea of what the ships in James's navy looked like, and you will see also that not only were people's clothes more colourful then than they are today, but that the ships were as well, at least when they had all their flags flying. The total cost of the standards for the 'Great Michael' was at least £72, and they must have been huge, for the St Andrew's cross required 22 ells of cloth and the one with the royal arms needed 33 ells of lining. All the ships also flew streamers of different colours, red, green, purple and yellow, and their tops and the sides of their *castles* were ornamented with designs and with coats-of-arms in colour. The 'Margaret' had, as an extra decoration, a rose at the end of her *bowsprit* – can you guess why? – which was also painted, so it is not surprising to know that Andrew Chalmers the painter earned nearly £140 for work on the King's ships alone between 1511 and 1513.

James now had the fleet which he wanted, and if this was a story book instead of a history book we could make up wonderful adventures for it under the command of Sir Andrew Wood or even of James himself. But though we cannot do that, there is one odd thing that we must notice, which is that the ships just vanish from history – 'the fleet vanishes into fairyland', as a famous historian said. We shall see what really happened in the last chapter.

James IV and England

Those of you who have already learned some Scottish history in school or who have read story books of Scottish history at home will know that much of it is taken up with wars with England and fighting on the Borders. Any of the famous ballads, such as 'The Battle of Otterburn', 'Kinmont Willie', 'Jock o' the Side' and 'Jamie Telfer' will give you a good idea of what this was like.

The reign of James IV was very similar to the reigns of the other Scottish kings in this way, but there was one important difference. In 1503 James married Margaret Tudor, daughter of Henry VII, and there was then a splendid chance for the two kingdoms to settle down to a long period of peace. As we know, this did not happen, but the marriage did have one very important result exactly one hundred years later. Do you know what this was?

THE MARRIAGE OF THE THISTLE AND THE ROSE

You would think that a marriage between the ruling families of such old enemies as Scotland and England would be almost impossible, but there were several reasons why both James and Henry thought that it would be a good idea. Each of them wanted peace so that their countries could develop and become stronger: Henry wanted to be sure that England would be safe from attack in the future, especially in wars with France; he also hoped that one day Scotland might be united with England, and

75

James saw that it was just possible that he might become King of England himself.

But, though both Kings were in favour of the marriage, there were several obstacles in its way. For one thing, James was then twenty-five years old and Margaret was only nine. Then, too, some of the English nobles feared that it might bring England under the rule of a Scots king, and, lastly, James and Margaret were third cousins, and so were within the *prohibited degrees* – that is, they were too closely related to be married. However, most of these difficulties could be overcome. The marriage was not to take place till Margaret was older; Henry assured his nobles that England would never be ruled by a Scots king, because it was the larger country and would absorb the smaller; and permission for the marriage to take place (called a *dispensation*) was obtained from the Pope.

The next thing to be done, of course, was for ambassadors from Scotland to go to the English court and make arrangements for the marriage and for a peace treaty. James chose the Archbishop of Glasgow, the Bishop of Moray and the Earl of Bothwell to do this important business. William Dunbar was one of the party which accompanied them, and he was so impressed with what he saw that he wrote a poem about London, in which he praised it as 'the flower of cities all'. Everything went smoothly. The marriage was fixed for the autumn of 1503, Margaret's *dowry* was to be £10,000 and her allowance was fixed at £1,000 Scots. (A Scots pound was then between one-third and one-quarter of the value of an English pound.) As a marriage gift she was to get Ettrick Forest, the castles of Doune, Newark and Stirling, the palaces of Methven and Linlithgow, the Earldom of Dunbar, the shires of Linlithgow and Stirling and various other pieces of land besides. The day after this was arranged there was a ceremony at' which Margaret promised to accept James as her husband, and the Earl of Bothwell accepted her as the King's wife; after which the trumpeters played 'in the best and most joyfullest manner', as one of the heralds wrote afterwards. The most important part of this meeting was the drawing up of a *treaty* of *perpetual* peace, and this was done so carefully that it seemed to cover every possible thing that might cause trouble between the two kingdoms. It even said that Scotland could help her old ally France against England – as long as the King of Scots did not actually invade England.

On 8 July Margaret said good-bye to her father (her mother had died some months before) and, under the care of the Earl of Surrey and his Countess, and accompanied by a large *retinue*, she set out for Scotland. All along her route nobles and gentlemen turned out as escorts for the Queen-to-be, and there were receptions in every town through which she passed, while, at the same time, tremendous preparations were set afoot in Scotland. Improvements were made and new building was pushed on at Stirling and the new palace of Holy-roodhouse, and, in the latter, in the Queen's chamber, a total of £937 10s. was spent on buying and making up cloth-of-gold, red and blue velvet and crimson cloth into the roofs and hangings for beds, for hangings in the chamber itself and for the lining of a smaller room. Cushions and carpets were also purchased, as were feather beds (and the feathers to stuff them!) pillows, sheets and blankets; sixteen tapestries depicting woodland scenes were bought at a cost of nearly £60, and five chairs of state costing £36 were brought all the way from Bruges.

As the Queen and her escort came nearer Scotland messengers were sent out reminding all the important

The Queen's Chamber, Holyroodhouse

people in the country to prepare for the marriage, while similar preparations were made in the court. In the year before his marriage, James himself got twelve gowns and sixteen ordinary coats, and the members of the court were also supplied with the materials for new clothes. Lord Hamilton got 16 ells of white damask, and Sir Alexander Bruce and Sir John Sinclair each got the same length of crimson velvet and black velvet, while other members of the king's household got tan or crimson satin or blue damask, with scarlet or black hose. No expense was spared to make the wedding a memorable occasion, and, when dressed up, the courtiers must have looked as brilliant as a bed of flowers.

Margaret[1] arrived in Scotland on 1 August, and, three days later, at Dalkeith, she met King James for the first

[1] See plate facing page 24.

78

time. It seems odd to us that two people who were going to be married should not meet at all until a few days before the actual wedding, but, of course, this often happened in those days. James rode out from Edinburgh accompanied by forty of his gentlemen and met the princess and her escort at the castle. No doubt Margaret had wondered what her future husband would be like and James seems to have tried hard to make her feel at home, as well as showing the Earl and Countess of Surrey and all the rest of the escort that they were welcome too. A day or two later he paid her another visit, and, after supper, he played to the company on the *clavichord* and the *lute*, and Sir Edward Stanley and a Scottish gentleman sang solos and a duet.

A lute

The Queen's entry into Edinburgh was the occasion of great rejoicing, as you may imagine. The King, dressed in a jacket of cloth-of-gold bordered with purple velvet, a doublet of violet

A clavichord

79

satin and scarlet hose, met her half-way, and Margaret mounted behind him on a *palfrey* on which they rode into the city, surrounded by the nobles and gentlemen of both countries, all dressed almost as finely as the King. *Pageants* had been specially arranged in honour of the day, and the company were first entertained by a *joust* between two knights in a field outside the walls, and then by a company of angels singing in a wooden gatehouse, one of whom presented the keys of the capital to Margaret. A stage had been put up in the centre of the town and three little plays were presented on it. Finally, they came to another gatehouse, on which were four thrones, one for each of the four Virtues – Justice, Force, Temperance and Prudence – under which they passed to a service in Holyrood Abbey. John Young, the Somerset Herald, who was a member of the English party, described all these happenings, and he says:

> 'The town of Edinburgh was in many places hung with tapestries, the houses and windows were full of lords, ladies, gentlewomen and gentlemen, and in the streets were so great a *multitude* of people without number that it was a fair thing to see. The ... people were very glad at the coming of the Queen; and in the churches of the town ... the bells were rung for *mirth*.'

The next day, 8 August, James and Margaret were married in Holyrood Abbey. Let us see if we can picture the marriage as it appeared to John Young, who later wrote a very careful account of it. The Queen entered the Abbey and stood near the font, with the Archbishop of York on her right hand and the Earl of Surrey on her left. She was dressed in a robe of white damask edged and lined with crimson velvet, and she wore also a gold collar encrusted with jewels and a long *coif* below the crown which had been specially made for her by an Edinburgh goldsmith out of thirty-five coins. Her train was carried

Holyrood Abbey today

by the Countess of Surrey, who, like her husband, was dressed in cloth-of-gold. Behind them stood the English ladies, two and two with the ladies of Scotland; the English party stood on the left of the church and the Scots on the right. The King was accompanied by his brother, the Archbishop of St Andrews, by the *Steward,* the *Chamberlain,* the *Constable,* the *Marshal* and their staffs, and by many other nobles, knights and gentlemen. He was dressed in a gown of white damask bordered with gold, a crimson jacket with black cuffs, a *doublet* of cloth-of-gold, scarlet hose, and a bonnet of black cloth in which there was a rich ruby. The service was performed by the Archbishop of Glasgow, and we can imagine for a moment the colour and magnificence of the scene, with the light falling from the Abbey windows on the many-coloured gowns and hoods, on the cloth-of-gold and scarlet and crimson, on the silks and satins, the damask and *camlet*, and on the chains and the collars of gold.

The wedding was followed by nearly a week of different entertainments, dancing and singing, conjuring and acrobatics, but especially *jousting* in the courtyard of the Palace, for which 180 new spears had been provided. It was watched by the King and Queen and the courtiers from the windows and from seats which had been specially erected for the occasion. There was one amusing incident not long after the wedding, when the Countess of Surrey and her daughter clipped the King's beard for him, as it was rather long, and for this service the Countess got a present of 15 ells of cloth-of-gold costing £330 and her daughter the same length of damask gold costing £180. Surely this must be a record payment for hair-cutting! The King also made forty-one new knights and gave them to the Queen, saying, 'These are your knights'; at the same time, Lord Hamilton was made the Earl of Arran, Lord Graham the Earl of Montrose and Lord Kilmaurs the Earl of Glencairn. This ceremony ended the festivities.

I wonder if by now you have found out just why this wedding was so important? It is because, exactly one century later, Scotland and England were united under the great-grandson of James and Margaret, who became King James VI of Scotland and I of England. If only the hundred years between could have been peaceful ones, both Scotland and England would have gained such a lot and missed such disasters! But, alas, only ten years after the treaty of perpetual peace had been signed, it was broken. Scotland suffered her greatest defeat and lost her King and many of her greatest and best on the battlefield of Flodden.

Obviously, something must have gone wrong with the friendship between the countries which had started in the year of James and Margaret's marriage, and we must try to find the causes of the trouble.

First of all, when Henry VII died in 1509 he was succeeded by his son Henry VIII, who, as you may know, was quite a different sort of person from his father. Henry VII was always anxious to avoid war if he could, but Henry VIII was hot-headed and impulsive, eager to 'win his spurs' as a general, and especially anxious to get back the province of Gascony from France, as it had once been an English possession – and Scotland, as you know, was France's old ally.

Then, there was the ill-feeling over the *legacy* which Prince Arthur had left his sister Margaret. It had not been handed over by Henry VII, and now Henry VIII also refused to give it up.

In 1507 there was trouble on the Borders again, when Sir Robert Ker, a Scottish *Warden of the Marches*, was killed by three Englishmen. Only one of the three was punished by the English King, and though two of the Warden's men killed the second one, Henry made no attempt to punish the third, who was the chief culprit.

Finally, in 1511, as you remember, came the capture of the 'Lion' and the 'Jenny Pirwin' and the death of Andrew Barton. James claimed that the English admiral had committed a crime by attacking his ships and killing his captain, but Henry VIII replied that kings should not quarrel over the fate of pirates, and this answer made James very angry.

These things all spoiled the friendship between the two countries, but they were not serious enough to cause war.

83

The real cause was the attack on France made by England in 1513, which was carried out because King Henry had joined a group of other countries in the Holy League, which was trying to drive the French out of Italy. In 1512 an ambassador from France arrived at the Scottish court to ask for James's help, and the King promised to do what he could. Of course, you remember that he was allowed to do this by the treaty of 1502, and war might not have begun at all if James had only loaned the French King his fleet, as he had been asked to do. But, when Henry sailed over to France in the middle of 1513, James not only sent about six of his ships to the French King, but also ordered his army to muster as well. He had decided that he must invade England.

In the middle of August the big guns were moved from Edinburgh Castle, each one drawn by thirty-six oxen with eight or nine drivers, and, as usual, accompanied by about twenty workmen armed with spades, picks and shovels and two ropes, one to help to pull the cannon uphill and the other to act as a brake going down. Loads of cannon balls and a string of powder carts went with the

Norham Castle, Northumberland

84

seventeen guns that set off for the Borders, but, unluckily for James and the Scottish army, many of the experienced gunners had been sent to the fleet, and were then on their way to France. The King left Edinburgh for the last time about 19 August and joined his army in Berwickshire, where most of it had collected.

Having crossed into England, James besieged and captured Norham and two other castles, but the weather was bad and there was plague in the army, and he probably felt that he had done all he could to help France. He had hoped that the news of his invasion would force the English King to return from France, but Henry had left the Earl of Surrey to look after the Borders while he was away, and now the Earl was advancing with an army of about 20,000 men – about the same size as the Scottish one. What would you have done in James's place – waited

The Earl of Surrey

85

to fight, or gone back to Scotland and perhaps invaded again when the English army had gone? Surrey was afraid that James would go back without a battle, so he sent him a challenge to a battle on 9 September, and the English admiral, who was with the army, also sent a message saying that, if James wanted revenge for the death of Andrew Barton, now was his chance! Surrey knew James well enough to be sure that he would accept this challenge, and so he did. He took up a strong position on Flodden Hill and waited for Surrey to appear.

Now, to understand what happened next, you must look at the map on page 87. You will see there that the English army first appeared to the south of the Scottish one, but when the Earl of Surrey saw what a strong position James had chosen, he led his army across the River Till, marched north, and then crossed the river again farther up, at Twizel Bridge and at Heton. This was a very clever move by the English commander, as his army now blocked the way back to Scotland. Meanwhile, Pitscottie tells us, Robert Borthwick, the Scots' master gunner, asked James's permission to destroy Branx Bridge by gunfire, but James refused, saying that he wanted a fair fight between the armies. Surrey then advanced to try to get his army on to the top of Branxton Hill, but James saw the danger, ordered the guns to be harnessed up, and, hidden by a cloud of smoke from burning rubbish, the whole Scottish army moved quickly to take up the position which Surrey had wanted. There, arranged in five divisions, they waited for the English.

As soon as the armies were within range, the artillery opened fire, but, as the Scots guns were on the hillside above the English army, many of their shots flew right over the heads of the advancing soldiers and did no harm, while nearly every shot fired by the English gunners hit

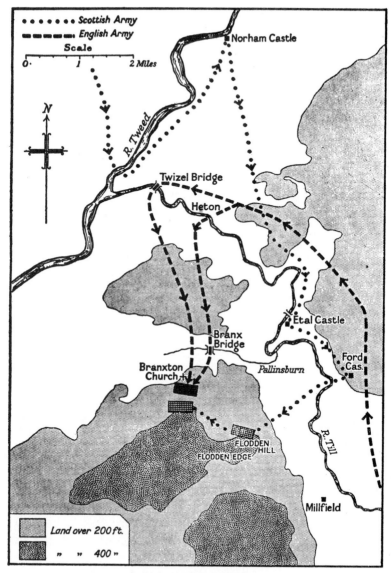

Scottish Army

English Army

Scale

0   1   2 Miles

N

R. Tweed

Norham Castle

Twizel Bridge

Heton

Branx Bridge

Branxton Church

Etal Castle

Pallinsburn

Ford Cas.

R. Till

FLODDEN HILL

FLODDEN EDGE

Millfield

Land over 200 ft.

„   „   400 „

Map of Flodden campaign

87

Artillery in action

its mark. James therefore ordered his army to advance, and the Scots, kicking off their shoes to get a better grip of the slippery ground, and with their fifteen-foot spears at the ready, came down the hill. The English right wing was the first to meet them, and were saved only by the arrival of the cavalry, which came across to their aid, but soon both front lines met face to face, and a battle of desperate fury began. Both sides fought fiercely and almost silently, but soon it was plain that the English eight-foot *bill* was a better weapon than the Scottish spear, and, when the spears were broken, swords were no match at all for the much longer bill. Nevertheless, the struggle went on grimly, the Scots, 'strong and great men that would not

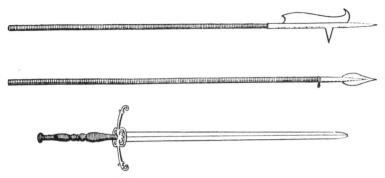

A bill, a spear and a two-handed sword

fall when four or five bills struck on them at once', being determined not to lose the day. But, as darkness began to fall, both wings of the Scottish army were defeated, and at last the centre itself broke before the English attacks.

What had happened to James? At the beginning of the

Armed men of the sixteenth century

Old drawing of the battle of Flodden

battle he told his nobles that he was going to lead his men in person, and, in spite of their protests, he took up his position in the front ranks. There, we may believe, he fought as bravely as any, killing five of his opponents with his spear before it broke, and fighting his way forward to within a few feet of where the English commander sat in his chariot directing the battle. There, somewhere in the thick of that struggling mass of men, pierced by an arrow and deeply wounded by a bill, he must have died. When night finally put an end to the fighting, about half the Scottish army lay dead beside their King, including his son, the Archbishop of St Andrews, two bishops, two abbots, the French Ambassador, nine earls, fourteen lords and possibly one member of every important family in Scotland.

Many years after the battle a lady called Jane Elliot

wrote the words of a lament for Flodden, which has become one of the most famous Scottish songs ever composed. As you probably know, the tune is often played by the pipers at military funerals and at Armistice Day services.

> 'I've heard them lilting at our ewe-milking,
> Lasses a' lilting before dawn o' day;
> But now they are moaning on ilka green loaning –
> The Flowers of the Forest are a' wede away.'

CONCLUSION

It would be a pity to end this story with a tragedy, though you can see for yourselves that the battle of Flodden was indeed a national disaster, one of the worst that Scotland has ever suffered. The King was dead and the heir to the throne was only seventeen months old; of the great lords who might have helped to govern the country it is said that only four remained; the whole south of Scotland waited with terror the advance of the English army which they were sure would follow the battle. The invasion of England had not even succeeded in helping France as it was supposed to do, by forcing Henry VIII to return, and the Scottish fleet, badly led by the Earl of Arran, had wasted time in an attack on Carrickfergus and had been of no use to the French at all. The 'Great Michael' was purchased for 40,000 *livres* by Louis XII, but mouldered away in a French port, and though we catch brief glimpses of the 'James' and 'Margaret' again in 1516, the fleet of which James was so proud and on which he spent so much money seems to disappear from the pages of history. Without doubt, Scotland was in a much worse position in 1513 than she had been a quarter of a century before, when James became her king.

But, though 1513 was such a disastrous year for Scotland, we must not think of that alone, but remember to look at the whole of James's reign as part of a much longer period of history. The reigns of the first three Jameses were very stormy ones, and those of James V and Mary, Queen of Scots, were to be no better, therefore the twenty-five years of James's reign were of great importance to the country and to its people. Though they were not completely peaceful years, we know that they were quiet enough for the King to establish good order and firm government, to do something to make the Highlands and the Borders less unruly, to build a navy and to become a person of some importance in Europe. Without this peace which James managed to give Scotland, the ideas of the Renaissance could not have spread as they did, there might have been no introduction of printing, no foundation of the College of Surgeons and of Aberdeen University, and, worst of all, perhaps none of the wonderful poetry of Henryson and Dunbar. Finally, the King's marriage to Margaret Tudor led in the long run to the Union of the Crowns in 1603, which, in turn, led gradually to peace between Scotland and England.

Thus, though no doubt you feel that you prefer the comfort and safety of the twentieth century to the hardships and dangers of the sixteenth, I wonder if you now agree that the reign of James IV was one of the most interesting periods of Scottish history?

HOW DO WE KNOW?

Have you ever wondered how history books are written? There is really only one correct way, and that is to read all the *sources* that one can, and then decide on two things – first, what really happened, and second, the best way to tell the story. The sources which are most useful to us are diaries, letters, charters, memoirs, inscriptions, laws and accounts, as well as the actual history books written at or just after the time that we are studying, and the biographies of people of the period. Of course, sometimes we find that two writers describe the same event in quite different ways, so we then have to make up our minds if one is trying to give a false picture for a special reason – you remember that Don Pedro was trying to arrange a marriage between James and a Spanish princess, and so made Scotland seem to be a very attractive place, and the King a very fine and wealthy person. So, you see, the more sources we have the better; and if we can get the same story from several different sources, then we can be pretty sure that it is true.

The easiest way to get information is, of course, to read actual history books or 'Lives' (which we would call biographies), and you already know the names of two people who wrote about James's reign, John Major and Robert Lindsay of Pitscottie. John Major was born in 1470 and his history was published in 1521, but, though much of his early life was spent in France, his book is a very reliable one, and he does not repeat some of the silly stories which appear in older histories. Our second writer, Robert Lindsay, was born in 1500, and so he was able to get information from people who knew all about James's reign. In fact, he tells us that he was helped by John Major and Sir Andrew Wood and others, but, strangely enough, his history is not very reliable. Another rather unreliable one was written by Hector Boece, the first Principal of Aberdeen University; but another of his books tells us a lot about the life of Bishop Elphinstone, so we are grateful for that. Finally, though George Buchanan's history was written long after James's death, we would be foolish not to consult the work of a writer who was born in 1506 and whose account of our period is believed to be reliable.

Of course, it would be very unfair to write about matters concerning both England and Scotland without seeing what the English historians had to say, and for this purpose Edward Hall's CHRONICLE is the best. This is partly a translation of a history written by Polydore Vergil, an Italian who lived in England in Henry VII's reign, and it is a very fair account. Also, the fullest description of James's marriage to Margaret is

A picture from Hector Boece's History

that written by John Young, Somerset Herald, who accompanied the English party to Scotland. You can read the whole description in a collection of historical records made by John Leland, who was Henry VIII's chaplain.

Another of the sources that was used to make this book was one of the big volumes containing the Acts of the Scottish Parliament. Perhaps you think that these Acts would be very dry and uninteresting, but, though some of them would be difficult for you to understand, there are many other very interesting ones too – acts about the *warding of the marches*, about holding *wappinshaws* and fairs, about weights and measures and exorbitant prices, about catching salmon and killing wolves and about rooks building in trees. We can read how Sir Andrew Wood was to be allowed to build a castle, and how another castle with the dismal name of Gloom was to be called Castle Campbell in future; and there are Acts about trade to Europe, about the clothes that one should wear and the weapons that one should have, and Acts against playing football (because it interfered with archery practice) and even one about a new way of making salt!

Two other sources of the period have got difficult Latin names. They are called *Rotuli Scaccarium regum Scotorum* and *Compota Thesauriorum regum Scotorum*, but we will call them the Exchequer Rolls and the Treasurer's Accounts for short. From both of them we can find out a great deal about the actual events of the time, about life in the court, about occupations and amusements, about dress and food, argiculture and commerce. For example, all the information about Andrew Simpson came from the Exchequer Rolls, and the Treasurer's Accounts supplied many facts about the court, the navy and about James's artillery. These Accounts are really one of our best sources, for the Treasurer had to deal with the purchase of clothing for the royal family and for the court, the buying of horses and equipment, the repair of royal buildings and the cost of new buildings, with gifts to people and with offerings in church, with the payment of officials and the entertainment of *ambassadors*, and, as we know, the cost of James's new navy and artillery.

Just as we were able to collect a lot of facts from the Acts of Parliament, so we can find out a great deal from the burgh records, especially about the life of the people in towns and about the trade of the country. Of course, we learned a lot from Andrew Halyburton's ledger, but we need the burgh records too, for they tell us about such things as the loading of ships, the collection of customs, the holding of markets, the price of ale, the sale of poultry, the tax on flour and the letting of mills. Along with these are the convictions of bakers for selling under-weight cakes, announcements of people being '*put to the horn*' for murder and sentenced for quarrelling, about the appointment of schoolmasters, the setting up of shooting butts for archery practice, the cleaning of Leith harbour, the building of a tower on Edinburgh's old Tolbooth, the re-pair of the church steeple at Peebles, and even the cost of oil for the town clock!

Letters written at this period helped also, and we are lucky to have a great many letters written between 1505 and 1513 between Scotland and the countries of Europe. The King of Denmark was James's uncle, so it

The Sword of State, given to James by Pope Julius II

is natural to find that there were more than thirty written from each King to the other, especially as the Danish King was trying to borrow some of James's ships to help him against attacks by Sweden. The importance of the Church at this time is shown by the sixty-five letters from Scotland to the Pope: and, of course, there were a lot between Scotland and England and Scotland and France, not counting smaller numbers between Scotland and such unlikely places as Poland and Hungary. Patrick Paniter, James's secretary, must have been kept busy! From these letters it is easy to see that Scotland was quite an important country in James's reign, and from them we can trace the story of the quarrel between England and Scotland which led at last to the battle of Flodden. One other letter should not be forgotten – that of Don Pedro de Ayala – but we have already seen how important that one is to a study of James's reign.

Lastly, there is the poetry of Henryson and Dunbar, which often gives us word-pictures of what we have already learned from our study of the period – the description of the food eaten by the country mouse and the town mouse; the leper, with begging bowl and *clapper* going to the hospital at the town's end; the *cadger* who finds a dead fox and decides to make mittens of its fur rather than sell its pelt to Flanders; the

Panels from the hospital founded by Patrick Paniter

lords and ladies in their silks and finery, which have really been paid for by the work of the peasants. These, and many other descriptions, make it easier for us to imagine life as it was in the days of James IV.

Only those books and documents which have been used to make this story have been mentioned in this section, but there are many others from which more information could have been collected. Perhaps when you are older you would like to study this period in more detail, and then you would learn all about these other sources of information and read them for yourselves.

THINGS TO DO

1. Make a drawing of the battle of Sauchieburn or of the scene in the mill when the King was killed.

2. Imagine that you are an ambassador from a foreign country, just arrived in Scotland for the first time. From the information given on pages 2–6 write a letter to your king, describing Scotland and her people.

3. Make a drawing of the arrival of the King's party at Linlithgow Palace for the Christmas celebrations, or of the scene in the hall of the Palace afterwards (pages 10–13).

4. Make up a programme of entertainments for Christmas week, as though you had been chosen to be the Abbot of Unreason.

5. Draw up an imaginary lease for Andrew Simpson's land on the Grange of Bothkennar, stating all the services that he had to give, how much land he was to have, and what his rent would be for the year (pages 19–20).

6. If you live in a burgh try and see a copy of the burgh charter and make a note of all the rights and privileges which have been granted to the town.

7. Go to your local library and ask to see the oldest known plan of your town or city, and make a copy of it in your note-book.

8. See if there are any entries about a plague in your town records, and write down what they say about it, or write a report on the one which attacked Edinburgh from 1498–1500, as if for a local newspaper.

9. Make a drawing of the Abbot of Tungland flying from the battlements of Stirling Castle (page 48–9).

10. Find out what you can about other kinds of guns which were used at this time, as well as the ones mentioned in the book, and make drawings of a few of them.

11. Make a drawing of Sir Andrew Wood's fight with Sir Stephen Bull in 1490 (page 62–3).

12. Imagine that you are a Scottish merchant and write a friendly letter to Andrew Halyburton, asking him to send you a list of goods from Antwerp, explaining why you want some of them (page 65–8).

13. Read one of the ballads mentioned on page 75 and re-write the story in your own words.

14. Make a list of all the things which you think might have been mentioned in the treaty of perpetual peace which was made between England and Scotland when James and Margaret were married.

15. Paint a picture of the Queen's entry into Edinburgh, or of the scene in Holyrood Abbey (pages 79–81).

16. Write a letter as if from the King of France to James in 1513, asking his help to fight against the English and explaining why France was being attacked by England at this time.

17. With the help of the illustrations in this book, make a drawing of the Scots army advancing down the hill at Flodden, or of the hand-to-hand fighting.

18. Learn the tune and the words of 'The Flowers of the Forest.'

THINGS TO DO TOGETHER

1. Read the story of the nobles' meeting at Lauder in 1482 and make up a little play about it, using the actual words of the speakers as much as possible.

2. Write and act a conversation between Henry VII and his nobles discussing the proposal that James should marry Margaret.

3. Act the events in Linlithgow Palace on the eve of Christmas Day, with members of the class taking the parts of the King, nobles, servants and entertainers.

4. Make up a play about the council of war between James and his nobles before Flodden, including among the characters the King, Lord Hume and the Earl of Huntly (who were to command the left wing), the Earls of Lennox and Argyll (who commanded the right), Robert Borthwick, the master gunner, James's son Alexander, the Archbishop of St. Andrew; and various messengers.

5. Collect as many pictures as you can of places which were important in the reign of James IV and make them into a frieze for your class room. (Modern pictures will do quite well if you cannot find older ones.) Write a little note for each picture to explain what connexion it has with his reign.

6. Try and find some other books on the reign of James IV and see what else you can learn about his reign, such as the stories of Perkin Warbeck and of the Lollards of Kyle, and write them in your note-books in your own words.

GLOSSARY

to abdicate: to give up the Crown or some other special office
address: the way a person carries himself
allegory: story which has a hidden meaning
ambassador: representative sent by one country to another
anatomy: study of the structure of the body
aqua vitae: 'water of life' or alcohol
arable: land suitable for crop-growing
Aragonese: language spoken in the old northern province of Spain
avaricious: greedy
balk: unploughed piece of land dividing one rig from another
to become: to look well on someone
bellman: town crier
bill: combined spear and battleaxe
bittern: marsh bird like a heron
bombard: heavy cannon used for sieges
booth: covered stall in a market
bowsprit: spar fastened to the bow of a sailing ship, to which are
    fastened ropes and sails.
brander: gridiron
broken men: outlaws
buckram: coarse linen cloth
bull: document issued by the Pope
burgess: inhabitant of a burgh
burgh: town which has been given certain rights by a king or noble
cadger: dealer or hawker
calibre: inside diameter of a gun
camlet: light cloth used for cloaks
canopy: covering or roof over a bed or a throne
capon: fowl specially fattened up for eating
Castilian: language spoken in the centre and south of Spain
casting: metal article shaped in a mould
castle: fighting tower on a medieval sailing ship
cauldron: large pot with a hoop handle
cavalcade: troop of riders
chalice: goblet or cup used in Church
Chamberlain: superintendent of the royal household
chandelier: support for lights hanging from a ceiling
charger: large flat dish

charter : document setting out rights or privileges granted by a king or noble

chequered cloth : cloth having a pattern of squares

clapper : hand rattle used by lepers to warn people of their coming

clartier : dirtier

classics : writings which people agree to be the finest of their kind

clavichord : stringed instrument with a keyboard, like a piano

coif : close cap covering the whole head

Constable : commander of the army in medieval times

corpse present : a peasant's second best animal or best garment, taken by the Church when he died

craft : group of workmen of the same trade

crossbow : bow fastened to a stock which held the arrow, whose string was drawn tight by a machine called a 'mill', and which was fired by a trigger

crucible : container used for melting any substance

cupples : beams used in house construction

dais : raised platform

damask : table linen or other woven material

diocese : bishop's district

dispensation : exemption from a penalty or duty commanded by church law

doublet : close-fitting body-garment

dowry : gift brought by the bride to her husband

ell : old measurement of length: 45 inches

ewer : water-jug

falconer : keeper and trainer of hawks

falcon : bird used for hunting: a small cannon

fire-ball : ball filled with materials which would burn easily

flail : wooden implement for threshing grain

forecastle : short raised deck at the bow of a ship

fustian : thick twilled cotton cloth

girdle : flat iron plate for baking

goblet : metal or glass drinking cup

grassum : sum of money paid by a person who takes a lease of land

Gregorian chant : kind of music named after Pope Gregory

gun-port : port-hole in a ship through which a gun was fired

hackbutt : early kind of gun, like a musket

halbert : see bill

hand-culverin : small fire-arm

handspike: wooden lever tipped with iron for use with artillery

heriot: peasant's best beast, taken by his landlord when the peasant died

heron: long-legged wading bird

humane: compassionate

imposter: one who pretends to be someone else, a swindler

justice ayre: circuit journey made by a judge to try cases in different centres

lade: mill-stream

largesse: money or gifts given by a king or noble on special occasions

laver: washing basin

legacy: sum of money or articles left to someone in the will of a dead person

leper: person with a disease called leprosy

liard: old French coin

liberal: generous, open-handed

lime-pot: pot to hold lime which could be tipped over the heads of besiegers attacking a castle or anyone trying to board a ship

livery: the uniform worn by a servant

livre: old French coin, about the same value as a franc

lute: musical instrument like a guitar

mail gloves: gloves of iron or steel, part of a suit of armour

makar: poet

mantle: cloak

Marshal: important officer in the royal household who arranged ceremonies and processions

masquerading: pretending to be someone else

mazer: wooden drinking bowl

melter: workman who melted the iron for casting cannon

mether: drinking cup

midden: heap of rubbish

minstrel: singer or musician in medieval times

mirth: happiness or pleasure

monochord: musical instrument of one chord or string

monopoly: complete control of the trade in some commodity

mortar: container made of hard material for mixing ingredients

mortuary due: the same as corpse present

outfield: poor land not very suitable for crops

pageant: brilliant procession, or a play showing events in history

palfrey: saddle-horse, especially for ladies

pall: cloth held over some important person in a procession *peasant:* worker on the land

pedagogy: place where teaching is done.

penance: act done to show sorrow for a wrong that one has committed

perpetual: eternal

pestilence: epidemic of a fatal disease

petition: request

pitch: substance got from tar

pitcher: large earthenware drinking vessel with a handle or two ears

plainsong: music without bars, used in the Church since early times

platter: flat dish or plate

populous: thickly inhabited

porpoise: fish-like mammal of the whale family

porringer: small basin

prodigal: wasteful

prohibited degrees: Church laws passed to prevent closely-related people
    from marrying

precept: commands

Provost: head of a university college

puncheon: large cask for holding liquids

Pursuivant: officer in the College of Arms, under that of Herald

put to the horn: outlawed

quern: hand-mill for grinding grain

Regent: in medieval Scottish universities, an instructor who took
    students through their entire course

repletion: fullness

retinue: number of persons who are in attendance on a prince or great
    lord

rhetoric: art of persuasive or impressive speaking

rig: ridge, a portion of a field

sacrament: religious ceremony

saffron: orange-yellow substance used as colouring or flavouring

see: area ruled by a bishop or archbishop

serpentine: sixteenth-century cannon

Sheriff: chief officer of the king in a county or shire

sickle: reaping hook

sling: small cannon, another name for a culverin

solan goose: gannet

sources: writings of different kinds used in writing history

spit: bar for roasting meat before a fire

staple port: port through which all a country's trade was supposed to pass *stature:* height

statute and ordained: decreed and ordered

Steward: officer who managed the royal household

sturgeon: large fish from which caviare is obtained.

subjection: to be under the control of someone

tableau: silent and motionless group of people arranged to represent a
scene

tapestry: fabric on which a design or picture is stitched, used for
covering walls or furniture

temperate: moderate

theology: study of the Christian religion

tolbooth: building where market tolls were collected and also used as a
goal

toll: tax or duty

top: platform on the mast of a ship, used in fighting

treaty: agreement between nations

trencher: wooden platter

trestle: wooden support for a table or bench

tron: weighing beam

vanguard: front division of an army

venison: deer meat

vennel: narrow lane in a town

vestment: official robe of a clergyman or official

wappinshaw: inspection of armed men made in medieval times

Warden of the Marches: guardian of a part of the Border between
Scotland and England

to winnow: to remove the chaff from grain

yeoman: retainer or attendant who carried out menial tasks

Yule: Christmas